rororo

rororo sprachen

Herausgegeben von Ludwig Moos

Die häufigsten Fehler im Englischen machen wir, weil die Muster unserer Muttersprache so mächtig sind. *Stop Making Mistakes* hilft Ihnen, von A bis Z die deutschen Fallstricke der englischen Sprache zu vermeiden. Mit Selbsttests, die Ihnen das Problem bewusst machen, Lektionen zum Verlernen des Fehlers und amüsanten Prüfungen werden Sie gegen das Fehlervirus immun. Sie lernen nicht nur, die tückischen „falschen Freunde" zu entlarven, sondern bauen Ihren Wortschatz zum sicheren Gebrauch in der Umgangssprache aus.

Robert Kleinschroth unterrichtet Englisch am Gymnasium und an der Universität Heidelberg. Zusammen mit Dieter Maupai hat er *La Conversation en s'amusant* (18873) und *Flüssiges Französisch* (61184) verfasst und außerdem *Sprachen lernen* (19110) geschrieben. Mit René Bosewitz hat er bei rororo sprachen mehr als zwanzig Bände zu *Business English* veröffentlicht.

Robert Kleinschroth

Stop Making Mistakes

Sprachfallen vermeiden von A bis Z

Rowohlt Taschenbuch Verlag

5. Auflage März 2011

Originalausgabe
Veröffentlicht im Rowohlt Taschenbuch Verlag GmbH, Reinbek bei Hamburg,
Oktober 2003

Umschlaggestaltung any.way, Barbara Hanke / Wiebke Buckow
(Illustration: Artworker Gerd Huss)
Layout Anne Drude
Satz Stone PostScript, QuarkXPress 4.11
Druck und Bindung CPI – Clausen & Bosse, Leck
Printed in Germany
ISBN 978 3 499 61567 2

FSC www.fsc.org MIX Papier aus verantwortungsvollen Quellen FSC® C083411

Das für dieses Buch verwendete FSC®-zertifizierte Papier *Classic* liefert Stora Enso, Finnland.

TROUBLE SPOT E

TROUBLE SPOT F

TROUBLE SPOT G

TROUBLE SPOT H

TROUBLE SPOT J

TROUBLE SPOT K

TROUBLE SPOT L

TROUBLE SPOT M / N

TROUBLE SPOT P

TROUBLE SPOT R

TROUBLE SPOT S

TROUBLE SPOT T

TROUBLE SPOT U

TROUBLE SPOT V

TROUBLE SPOT W

TROUBLE SPOT Z

LÖSUNGEN DER AUFGABEN

Dieses Buch hat drei Ziele. Es will Ihnen helfen, typische Fehler zu vermeiden, Ihren Sprachschatz zu erweitern, und Sie sollen dabei etwas zu lachen haben.
Es ist ein humorvolles Nachschlagewerk, ein Wiederholungskurs, ein Test- und Übungsbuch. Sie lernen und üben nicht nur mit kurzen Beispielsätzen, sondern mit vielen hundert sorgfältig ausgewählten *jokes* und witzigen Zitaten.
Sie kennen sicher schon einige der tückischen Sprachfallen, in die wir Deutsche immer wieder hineintappen: Eine Parkbank ist leider nicht *a park bank*; blamieren nicht *to blame* und *become a baby* heißt nicht ein Kind bekommen. Ich habe für Sie über hundert der häufigsten Wortschatzfallen ausgewählt, die in der Umgangssprache immer wieder zu peinlichen Missverständnissen führen.
Wie können Sie mit diesem Buch arbeiten? Die Probleme sind im ersten Teil alphabetisch deutsch-englisch angeordnet, im Anhang finden Sie das englisch-deutsche Stichwortverzeichnis. Jedes Problem gehen wir in drei beziehungsweise vier Schritten an.

1. TEST YOURSELF

Mit den Schnell- und Selbsttests prüfen Sie, ob Sie gegen die Sprachfalle gefeit sind. Wenn ja, gehen Sie zum amüsanten vierten Teil über oder lösen die Selbsttests quer durch das Buch, um nur dort tiefer einzusteigen, wo Sie auf ein Problem stoßen.

2. TROUBLESHOOT your English

In knapper und übersichtlicher Form erhalten Sie hier die Regeln, Anmerkungen und Beispiele, die Ihnen helfen, typische Sprachfallen künftig zu umgehen.

3. The specialist's CORNER

Die Ecke für Fortgeschrittene, die mehr wissen wollen, enthält wichtige Ausnahmen und Redewendungen. Wer den Selbsttest ohne Mühe löst, findet hier noch manches Merkwürdige.

4. JOKE YOUR WAY round trouble spots

Die vierte Sparte ist das Besondere an diesem Buch. Pfiffige Zitate und kurze *jokes* laden Sie ein, das erworbene Wissen zu testen und zu üben. Die Lösungen zu allen Tests und Übungen finden Sie im Anhang.
Viel Erfolg und Spaß bei der Lektüre.

1 Abteil(ung) – *compartment, department* oder *section*?

TEST YOURSELF : Right or Wrong?

	R	W
1. On a train: This is a first-class *section*. You've only got a second-class ticket.		
2. Don't ask me about our finances: that's my wife's *department.*		
3. Her husband is head of the finance *compartment* in the health department.		

TROUBLESHOOT your English

Abteil(ung)	*im Zug*	compartment
	in der Firma, Universität	department
	Ressort in der Behörde, Firma	section

The specialist's CORNER

Kaufhaus	department store
germanistische Abteilung	German department
Gesundheitsamt	health department
das ist das Ressort meiner Frau	that's my wife's department
Leiter des Finanzressorts /-referats	head of the finance section

JOKE YOUR WAY round trouble spots

1. "I'm sorry, Smith," said the director of the ______________ store to his assistant, "but being able to skate[1] around all nine of the ______________ completely blindfolded[2] does not qualify you for senior management[3]!"

2. Two men are sitting opposite each other in a train ______________. One man asks, "Have you given up smoking?" – "Quite right, sir. How did you notice?" – "Because you always stub out[4] your biscuits in the ashtray[5]".

2 **Aktion** ist nicht immer ***action***

TEST YOURSELF : What is *action* in German?

1. You must judge[6] people by their *actions*. ______________
2. Her son was *killed in action* in Iraq. ______________
3. The time has come *for action*. ______________

TROUBLESHOOT your English

action **= Aktion, Tat, Handeln**	
ein Mann der Tat	a man of action
eine Maschine in Aktion testen	test a machine in action
action **in juristischer Bedeutung**	
ein Gerichtsverfahren einleiten	take legal action (against someone)
jemanden verklagen	bring an action against

1 Rollschuh laufen 2 mit verbundenen Augen 3 höheres Management 4 ausdrücken 5 Aschenbecher 6 beurteilen

campaign / drive / operation = **Aktion** im Sinne von *Unternehmen*	
eine Rettungsaktion	a rescue operation
einen Feldzug führen gegen	start a campaign / drive against
einen Werbefeldzug starten	launch an advertising campaign
Wahlkampf	election campaign

JOKE YOUR WAY round trouble spots

1. Sticker during the Bush-Gore presidential ________________:
   THANK GOD ONLY ONE OF THEM CAN WIN!

2. An applicant[1] was interviewed for a marketing position. "What we are looking for," said the personnel manager, "is a man of ________________, a man with drive[2], determination[3] and courage, a man who never quits[4], who can inspire others, in short – a man who can pull the company's football team up from the bottom of the league[5]."

1 Bewerber 2 Energie 3 Entschlossenheit 4 aufgeben 5 Tabellenende

3 aktuell ist nicht *actual*

TEST YOURSELF : What is *actually* in German?

1. The *actual* state of affairs[1] is hopeless. __________
2. He runs[2] the company, but the *actual* owner[3] is his wife. __________
3. They open at 8.00 but the *actual* film doesn't start until 8.30. __________

TROUBLESHOOT your English

***aktuell* im Sinne von ...**	
zurzeit, gegenwärtig *auf dem neuesten Stand* *aktuellem Interesse*	current(ly) up to date topical
***actually* hat drei Bedeutungen**	
die *tatsächlichen* Zahlen Ist es *wirklich* wahr? Es war *eigentlich* eine ganz gute Zeit.	the actual figures Is that actually true? It was quite a good time, actually.

→ ***actually*** kann oft nicht übersetzt werden, wenn es eine Aussage ergänzt oder abschwächt.

1. I've known Paul for years. Since we were babies, *actually*.
2. I do *actually* think that things have improved (*übrigens*).
3. We had quite a good time, *actually*.
4. Well, *actually* you still owe me $100.

1 Stand der Dinge 2 leiten 3 Besitzer

The specialist's CORNER

aktuelle Ereignisse	current events
die tatsächlichen Zahlen	the actual figures
Ist es wirklich wahr?	Is that actually true?
die aktuellen Zahlen	the latest / up-to-date figures
von aktuellem Interesse	of topical interest
ein aktuelles Thema	a topical / important issue

JOKE YOUR WAY round trouble spots

Translate the German in brackets.

1. The Bible is wrong. (*In Wirklichkeit*) there were four wise men[1]. On the way to Bethlehem one of them said he knew a short cut[2].
2. Sign seen on a beach: Girls, please do not bother the lifeguard[3] unless you are (*tatsächlich*) drowning.
3. Why people hate Microsoft: As soon as a program is running properly, it is no longer (*aktuell*). They offer you an update that takes months to get used to.

1 die heiligen (drei) Könige 2 Abkürzung 3 Rettungsschwimmer

4 alle(s) ist nicht immer *all*[1]

TEST YOURSELF : Spot the mistakes and correct them

1. He rings me up *all* two days.
2. He gives her *all what* she wants.
3. We'll help *all who* are ready to help themselves.

TROUBLESHOOT your English

alle 3 Stunden / Meilen	every 3 hours / miles
alles, was	everything (that) / all (that)
alle, die (jene)	all those who
alle möglichen	all sorts of
Geld ist nicht alles.	Money isn't everything.
Nimm (alles), was du willst.	Take anything you like.

→ **MERKE** : anything = (irgend)etwas, etwas Beliebiges

The specialist's CORNER

Viele feststehende Ausdrücke muss man einfach lernen.

Mein Geld ist alle.	I've run out of money.
Er kann alles.	He can do anything.
alles oder nichts	it's all or nothing
alles zu seiner Zeit	all in good time
auf alles gefasst sein	be prepared for the worst
Ende gut, alles gut.	All's well that ends well.

1 Siehe auch *„ganz"*, Seite 67

JOKE YOUR WAY round trouble spots

1. Tact is thinking (*alles, was*) you say without saying (*alles, was*) you think.
2. Some people will believe (*alles*) if you whisper it to them. LOUIS B. NIZER
3. Self-control is when you go into a supermarket to buy a pint[1] of milk – and (*alles, was*) you buy is a pint of milk.
4. (*Alle möglichen*) computer errors are turning up now. You would be surprised to know the number of doctors who claim[2] they are treating pregnant men[3]. ISAAC ASIMOV
5. Have you heard about the Scotsman who married a girl born on 29 February? He only had to buy her a birthday present once (*alle vier Jahre*).

5 **allein** ist nicht immer ***alone***

TEST YOURSELF : Which phrase fits best?

alone • himself • by themselves • on their own

1. Of all the applicants[4] they ____________ had the right qualifications.
2. His secretary was on strike so he answered the letters ____________.
3. They need help. They can't solve this problem ____________.
4. Suddenly the doors seemed to open all ____________.

1 ein halber Liter Milch 2 behaupten 3 schwangere Männer 4 Bewerber

TROUBLESHOOT your English

allein im Sinne von ...	
einsam	lonely, lonesome
ohne Gesellschaft	alone
etwas selber tun	do it oneself
von allein	by oneself
etwas ohne Hilfe tun	do it by oneself / on one's own
auf sich allein gestellt sein	be on one's own

JOKE YOUR WAY round trouble spots

1. Waiter: Would you like a lemon with your tea?
   Client: No. I prefer to be (*allein*).
2. Then I found out that every time I put popcorn in my pancakes[1] they turn over (*von allein*).
3. A: I began business (*allein*). I had absolutely nothing but my intelligence.
   B: That sure was a small beginning!
4. I could have done the job (*allein / selber*) in twenty minutes, but as things turned out[2] I had to spend two days to find out why it had taken two managers three weeks to do it wrong.

1 Pfannkuchen 2 sich herausstellen

6 also – *also, therefore, so, then* oder *well*?

TEST YOURSELF : What is *also* in English?

1. *Also* blieb er zu Hause.	____________ he stayed at home.
2. Lassen wir's *also*.	Let's leave it ____________.
3. *Also*, wenn du mich fragst ...	____________, if you ask me ...
4. Ich denke, *also* bin ich.	I think, ____________ I am.
5. Sie spielt nicht nur gut, sie komponiert *auch*.	She not only plays well, but ____________ writes music.

TROUBLESHOOT your English

Deutsches *also* kann (je nach Funktion) bedeuten:		
SATZEINLEITUNG	FOLGERUNG	FAZIT
well, now	therefore	so, then

→ **MERKE**: *so* wird der Aussage vorangestellt, *then* wird nachgestellt. Einleitendes dt. *Also, ...* entspricht oft *Well, ...* oder *Now, ...*

Englisches *also* kann bedeuten:		
auch, ebenfalls	ferner, außerdem	also, deshalb, folglich

JOKE YOUR WAY round trouble spots

also • so • now

1. "____________ you're Tom's boss. I've heard him mention[1] your name so often, Mr Slavedriver[2]!"
2. Security officer: Look, there is poisonous[3] gas in this bottle. ____________ what steps would you take, if I dropped this bottle? Young scientist: Very large ones, sir!
3. Sign in a shop window: Our clothes not only make girls slim[4], they ____________ make men look round.

1 erwähnen 2 Sklaventreiber 3 giftig 4 schlank

7 ein **anderer** ist nicht immer ***another***

TEST YOURSELF : Right or Wrong?

	R	W
1. Sie ist *anders* als ihre Schwester. She's *other* than her sister.		
2. Er reiste am *anderen* Tag ab. He left the *other* day.		
3. Da ist eine ganz *andere* Sache. That's a completely *different* matter.		

TROUBLESHOOT your English

***(an)other* = andere** im Sinne von *weitere, restliche, übrige*	
Noch weitere Fragen?	Any other questions?
unter anderem	among other things
Er ist ein zweiter Einstein.	He is another Einstein.
Noch einen Tee bitte.	Another cup of tea, please.
die anderen	the others
***different* = anderer, anders** im Sinne von *verschieden*	
es kam ganz anders	things turned out very differently
Urlaub mal anders	a holiday with a difference
das ist was ganz anderes	that's a completely different matter
Ich möchte einen anderen Wein probieren.	I'd like to taste a different wine.

The specialist's CORNER

noch viele andere	many / plenty more
Ich hab's mir anders überlegt.	I've changed my mind.
anders ausgedrückt	to put it another way

➜ Vorsicht Falle

Er reiste am anderen Tag ab.	He left the next day.
Ich habe ihn neulich / vor kurzem getroffen.	I met him in town the other day / night.

JOKE YOUR WAY round trouble spots

different • other • another • the other day

1. Love is the illusion that one man is (*anders als*) the rest.
2. "Do you know a guy with one leg called Moloney?" – "No. What's the name of his (*anderen*) leg?"
3. "I think I am going mad, doctor. Every time I ask someone the time I get a (*andere*) answer."
4. "You can't resign[1]," said the circus manager to the human cannonball[2]. "Where would I get (*einen anderen*) man of your calibre?"
5. I have the feeling that my house isn't too solid. (*Neulich*) I saw termites wearing helmets.

1 zurück-, abtreten 2 menschliche Kanonenkugel

8 Arbeit(en) – *work* oder *works*?

TEST YOURSELF : What is it in English?

1. Tom, have you (*machen*) your (*Hausaufgaben*) yet?
2. I have bought my wife the complete (*Werke*) of Tolstoy.
3. There has been an accident at the (*Wasserwerk*).

TROUBLESHOOT your English

work (immer Einzahl) = **Arbeit**	
seine Hausaufgaben machen	do one's homework
die Hausarbeit (Arbeiten im Haus) machen	do the housework
die Arbeiten von Handwerkern	the work of craftsmen
eine schöne / ein schönes Stück Arbeit	a nice piece of work
Akkordarbeit; im Akkord arbeiten	do piecework
works (immer Mehrzahl) = **Werk, Werke**	
das Gas-, Wasserwerk	the gasworks, waterworks
die Werke Bachs	the works of Bach

➜ MERKE : 1. get a job — *eine Arbeit, Stelle bekommen*
2. do a job — *eine Arbeit tun*

JOKE YOUR WAY round trouble spots

Complete the jokes.

1. "I hate ________," said the newly-wed bride. "You make the beds and clean the floors. Then three months later you have to do it all again."
2. A secondary school student asked his teacher if a person should be punished for something he hadn't done. "Of course not," said the teacher. – "Good," said the boy. "I haven't done my ____________."
3. Tim: I've heard you applied for that ____________ at the film studio. How was the interview?
   Tom: Difficult. I had to ride a horse for three hours.
   Tim: And did you get the ______________?
   Tom: No, but the horse did.

9 Art ist nicht *art*

TEST YOURSELF : What is it in English?

1. The walls were hung with all (*Arten*) of works of (*Kunst*).
2. She doesn't mean to be rude[1] – it's just her (*Art*).
3. She's not the (*Art / Sorte*) of person to lie.

TROUBLESHOOT your English

***art* = Kunst**	
die schönen Künste	the fine arts
Kunstwerk	work of art
die Kochkunst	the art of cooking
***way* = Art und Weise, Wesen**	
auf seine Art	in his way
auf die(se) Art	(in) this way
gewinnende Art	winning way
***kind, sort* = Art, Gattung**	
alle möglichen Leute	all sorts of people
alles Mögliche	all sorts of things

➜ **MERKE** : *bedrohte (Tier-, Pflanzen-)Arten:* endangered species

JOKE YOUR WAY round trouble spots

Which word fits the context best?

kind • way • art • sort

1. Tact: the ____________ of saying nothing when there is nothing to say.
2. There are two ____________ of statistics, the ____________ you look up[2] and the ____________ you make up[3].

1 unhöflich sein wollen 2 nachschlagen 3 erfinden

3. The best __________ to remember your wife's birthday is to forget it once.
4. He had the __________ of face that makes you realise[1] God does have a sense of humour.

10 auch – *as well, also, so* oder *too*?

TEST YOURSELF : Right or Wrong?

	R	W
1. Adults[2] read Harry Potter and children also do.		
2. I like tennis, and I also like squash.		
3. He can't hear and he can hardly speak either.		

TROUBLESHOOT your English

Auf die Stellung im Satz kommt es an:

1. *also* wird meist vorangestellt

He is good-looking, and *also* rich.
It's my favourite restaurant and *also* hers.
It's my favourite restaurant and hers *also*.

2. *too* und *as well* werden nachgestellt, vor *too* steht Komma

Tom is good-looking, and rich, *too*.
Tom is good-looking, and rich *as well*.

3. *so* + Hilfsverb + Subjekt

Tom is good-looking and rich, *so is Tim*.
Tom runs an antique shop, *so does Tim*.

1 erkennen 2 Erwachsene

4. ***auch nicht*: either** oder **neither** nach negativer Aussage
Mary *won't go* and Peter *won't (go) either*. Mary *won't go* and Peter *won't* and *neither* will John.
5. ***sowohl als auch*: both ... and; as well ... as; not only ... but also ...**
Both mother and baby are doing well. He *not only* acts but *also* writes his own plays. The championship is open to amateurs *as well as* to professionals.

JOKE YOUR WAY round trouble spots

Which word fits best into the context?

too • so • also • neither • as well

1. I know we're going to be happy. You adore me and ____ do I.
2. "I've borrowed my neighbour's bagpipes[1]." – "But you can't play the bagpipes!" – "I know, but __________ can my neighbour if I have them!"

   Lucy: What well-developed[2] arms you have.
   Betty: Yes, I play a lot of tennis.
   Lucy: And you ride horseback, ___________, don't you.

1 Dudelsack 2 gut entwickelt

11 **aufstehen** ist nicht immer ***stand up***

TEST YOURSELF : Which expression fits best?

get up • stand up • rise

1. Thank God I haven't got to ______________ early tomorrow.
2. You'll get a better view of the match if you ______________.
3. Let's ______________ to welcome the President.
4. Early to bed and early to ______________ makes a man healthy, wealthy and wise.

TROUBLESHOOT your English

- **get up** und ***rise*** (nicht aber *stand up*): aufstehen aus dem Bett
- **rise**: sich erheben von Stühlen und Betten
- **stand up**: aufstehen von Sitzgelegenheiten, das Gegenteil von *sit down*
- **get up** kann die förmlicheren *rise* und *stand up* ersetzen

JOKE YOUR WAY round trouble spots

1. How to make a speech: (*steh auf*), speak up[1], shut up[2].
2. Boss: How can one person make so many mistakes in a single day? Secretary: I (*stehe auf*) early.
3. My formula for success is (*stehe auf*) early, work late, and strike oil[3]. PAUL GETTY
4. At the end of a presentation, the chairman (*erhob sich*) and said, "Your presentation has not left me any the wiser." The presenter retorted[4], "Perhaps not wiser, Sir, but better informed."

1 laut sprechen 2 den Mund halten 3 auf Öl stoßen 4 erwidern

12 Bank – *bench* oder *bank*?

TEST YOURSELF : Right or Wrong?

	R	W
1. Several people were fishing from the river *bank*.		
2. I had lost my key and had to sleep on a park *bank*.		
3. The sun disappeared behind a *bench* of clouds.		
4. Our boat struck a *sandbank*. One person fell overboard.		

TROUBLESHOOT your English

BANK {
bench: Sitzgelegenheit
bank: Geldinstitut

The specialist's CORNER

die Reservebank	the (substitutes') bench
Hinterbänkler	backbencher
Weder Banken noch Sitzgelegenheiten:	
Sandbank	sandbank
Wolkenbank	bank of clouds

JOKE YOUR WAY round trouble spots

1. My __________ just sent me a note that my account is overdrawn[1] again. I'm going to try another _________. They can't all be overdrawn.
2. A couple walking in the park noticed a young man and woman sitting on a _______, kissing passionately[2]. "Why don't *you* do that?" said the wife. "Honey," replied her husband, "I don't even know that woman!"
3. "I was injured[3] when I was in the football team." – "How?" "I fell off the _________."

1 mein Konto ist überzogen 2 leidenschaftlich 3 verletzt

13 **bei** ist nicht immer ***by***

TEST YOURSELF : The choice is yours

1.	Er nahm das Kind bei der Hand.	He took the child ______ the hand.
2.	Er hat ein Haus bei Berlin.	He has got a house ______ Berlin.
3.	Er starb bei einem Unfall.	He died ______ an accident.
4.	Ich war bei meinem Freund.	I was ______ my friend's.

TROUBLESHOOT your English

Präpositionen kann man oft nicht wörtlich übersetzen.
Am besten lernt man ganze Ausdrücke.

***bei* = by**	
bei Nacht / Tag / Tagesanbruch	at night / day / dawn
bei der Hand fassen	take by the hand
jemanden beim Namen nennen	call someone by (his *oder* her) name
bei weitem	by far

Nehmen Sie für *bei* im Sinne von
an, in der Nähe von sicherheitshalber *near.*

Ort und Zeit	
bei Berlin	near Berlin
beim Fenster	near / by the window
Umstand und Situation	
bei einem Unfall	in an accident
bei guter Gesundheit	in good health
bei jedem Wetter	in all weathers

Falsche Freunde – False Friends	
er ist bei der Post	he works *for* the post office
er ist beim Essen	he's having his dinner
bei einem Glas Wein	*over* a glass of wine
bei offenem Fenster	*with* the window open

JOKE YOUR WAY round trouble spots

at • in • near

1. A bank is a place where they lend you an umbrella[1] (*bei*) fair weather and ask for it back when it begins to rain. MARK TWAIN
2. A well-known American movie actress died (*bei*) an accident. On her gravestone[2] it read: "At last she sleeps alone."
3. I was born in Lowell, Massachusetts, and the explanation is quite simple. I wished to be (*bei*) my mother. JAMES MCNEILL WHISTLER
4. A man bought a parrot[3] (*bei*) an auction after some very brisk bidding[4]. "I hope this bird talks," he said to the auctioneer. "Does he talk? Who do you think has been bidding against[5] you for the past twenty minutes?"

1 Regenschirm 2 Grabstein 3 Papagei 4 lebhaftes Bieten 5 bieten gegen

14 bekommen – *become, get, obtain* oder *receive*[1]?

TEST YOURSELF : Right or Wrong?

	R	W
1. Light colours *become* you, Tina.		
2. Tony *became* a doctor.		
3. Waiter, can I *become* a steak?		
4. Can you *get* BBC World Service on your radio?		
5. My wife's *becoming* a baby.		
6. She *obtained* a letter from her ex-friend today.		
7. I managed to *obtain* the book I wanted.		

TROUBLESHOOT your English

bekommen	
ohne Zutun ***erhalten*** *receive / get* a letter	mit Mühe ***erlangen*** *obtain* a prize
***become, get* = werden, im Sinne einer Zustandsänderung**	
become vor Adjektiv oder Substantiv become rich / President of the USA	get vor Adjektiven get rich / better / worse

The specialist's CORNER

Dieser Hut steht dir.	This hat becomes you.
Der Fisch ist mir nicht bekommen.	The fish didn't agree with me.
Sie bekommt ein Kind.	She's having a baby.

JOKE YOUR WAY round trouble spots

***Get, receive* or *become*?**

1. An Italian prime minister should not think of getting married until he ______________ a steady job[2].

1 siehe auch „werden", Seite 180 2 Dauerstellung

2. The young man asked the beautiful girl to marry him. He mentioned that his father was 98 and very rich. She __________ his step-mother.
3. "I think I am going mad, doctor. Every time I ask someone the time I __________ a different answer."

15 (be)merken – *notice, realize* oder *remark*?

TEST YOURSELF : Make the right choice

noticed • realised • remarked

1. "I'm not my usual self tonight," __________ Tom. "Yes, I've __________ the improvement[1]," said Tina.
2. Did you hear about the policeman who gave out a hundred parking tickets[2] before he __________ he was at a drive-in movie[3]?

TROUBLESHOOT your English

bemerken	
mit dem Mund	remark; mention (erwähnen)
vorwiegend mit Auge oder Ohr	notice
mehr mit dem Verstand	realize / become aware of

Zum Teil überlappen sich die Bedeutungen von *notice, realize* und *become aware of*

→ Zwei Schreibweisen: *realise* oder *realize*

The specialist's CORNER

bemerken (mit dem Mund)	
bemerken, dass ...	mention that ...
Möchten Sie etwas bemerken?	Would you like to comment?
nebenbei bemerkt	by the way / incidentally

1 (Ver-)Besserung 2 Strafzettel 3 Autokino

JOKE YOUR WAY round trouble spots

Right or Wrong? | R | W

1. "Our economics professor talks to himself. Does yours?" "Yes, but he isn't *aware* it. He thinks we're listening!"
2. Have you ever *mentioned* how England wins the World Cup only under a Labour government? HAROLD WILSON
3. "Doctor, I was looking in the mirror this morning, and I *remarked* that one of my eyes is different from the other!" "Oh?" replied the doctor. "Which one?"

16 besonders – *special, specific* oder *particular*?

TEST YOURSELF : The choice is yours

1. I usually agree with her, but in this ________ case I think she's wrong.
2. She has her own ________ way of doing things.
3. She took ________ care not to damage the parcel.
4. You'll need a ________ tool to do that.

TROUBLESHOOT your English

special = für nicht alltägliche Sonder- und Extra-Dinge	
zu einem Sonderpreis anbieten	offer at a special price
eine Spezialfarbe für Böden	a special paint for floors
particular / specific **= für besondere Einzelfälle oder einzelne Elemente einer Serie**	
eine bestimmte Farbe vorziehen	prefer a particular colour
aus keinem besonderen Grund	for no particular reason
besondere Anforderungen	the particular demands (of a job)
eine spezifische Behandlung von Krebs	a specific treatment for cancer

JOKE YOUR WAY round trouble spots

1. Scotsman: Could I hire a horse, please?
   Farmer: Certainly, Sir. Any ____________ kind?
   Scotsman: A long one – there are five of us.
2. Sign in bar: We have a ____________ arrangement with the bank. They don't serve beer and we don't cash cheques.
3. Lizzie couldn't get a man however hard she tried. But one day a gypsy[1] sold her a ____________ Chinese love potion[2] for 50 pence – and it worked. A week later she married the Chinese Ambassador[3]

17 besuchen – *attend, go to see* oder *visit*?

TEST YOURSELF : Spot the mistakes and correct them

1. His son visits a very expensive private school.
2. Let's attend a James Bond film tonight.
3. My family goes to see the British Museum every year.

TROUBLESHOOT your English

einen Freund besuchen	go and / to see a friend	*umgangssprachlich*
zum Arzt gehen	go and / to see a doctor	*siehe* → MERKE
ein Museum besuchen	visit a museum	*Institutionen besuchen*
zur Schule gehen	go to school	*regelmäßiger Besuch*
Kurse besuchen	attend courses	*gehobener als* go to

→ MERKE:

- I'll go *and* see my mother. **Aber:** I went *to* see my mother. Steht *go* nicht in der Grundform, muss man *go to* see nehmen.
- *pay a friend a visit* ist gehobener als *go and / go to see a friend.*

1 Zigeuner 2 Liebestrank 3 Botschafter

JOKE YOUR WAY round trouble spots

What is it in English?

1. Did you hear about the dog that (*besuchte*) a flea circus[1] and stole the show?
2. I (*ging zu*) a lawyer and said, "I need a lawyer to represent me competently and fairly." He said, "Make up your mind[2]."
3. "I hear you went to Europe this year. Which countries did you (*besuchen*)?" – "I don't know. My husband bought the tickets."
4. Meetings that you chair[3] are infinitely better than those that you merely (*besuchen*).

18 bis – *as far as, by, till* oder *to*?

TEST YOURSELF : What is it in English?

1. Let's wait (*bis*) the rain stops.
2. He should have been here (*bis*) one o'clock.
3. May I see you home (*bis zu*) the bus stop?

TROUBLESHOOT your English

***bis* mit Zeitangabe**		***bis* mit Ortsangabe**	
till / until	*betont die Dauer*	to	*ist am häufigsten*
by	*letzter Termin*	as far as	*betont das Ziel*

- ***from ... to***: *From* Munich *to* Ulm it's about 100 kilometres.
  I work *from* Monday *to* Friday.
- ***by the time*** steht in Verbindung mit einem Verb:
  When will the book be ready *by*? – *By* the end of April.
  By the time this letter *reaches* you I will have left London.

1 Flohzirkus 2 entscheiden Sie sich 3 den Vorsitz führen, leiten

- ***as far as***: Ziel oder Teilziel ist betont:
  She gave me a ride *as far as* the station.

bis **mit Zahlen, Messwerten**	***bis*** **= außer, bis auf**
5 to 6 cars	except (for / that)
up to 10 degrees	with the exception of
count (up) to 20	all were present except Tom
as high as 5 metres	down to the last man

→ MERKE:

- *Except for* the cover the two books are the same.
  Bis auf den Einband sind die Bücher identisch.
  Ein vollständiger Satz wird jedoch mit *that* angeschlossen:
  She remembered nothing about him *except that* his hair was black.

JOKE YOUR WAY round trouble spots

1. You're not a star (*bis*) they can spell[1] your name in Karachi.
   HUMPHREY BOGART
2. I can't understand the fuss[2] over computer pornography. Surely everybody has seen a computer without clothes on (*bis*) now.
3. (*Bis*) a man can read women like a book he's too old to start a library.
4. Concorde travels at twice the speed of sound, which is fun, (*bis auf*) the fact that you can't hear the movie (*bis*) two hours after you land.
   HOWIE MANDEL

1 buchstabieren 2 Aufregung

19 Bitte sehr / bitte schön – four phrases in English

TEST YOURSELF : How would you react?

You're welcome • Go ahead • Here you are • (Yes), please

1. Another cup of tea?
2. May I use your phone?
3. Have you got an aspirin for me?
4. Thank you for helping me.

TROUBLESHOOT your English

Bitte ...	
als höfliche Aufforderung *um Wiederholung: „Wie bitte?"*	please (Endstellung) Pardon?
Reaktion ...	
auf eine Bitte um Gegenstände *auf eine Bitte, etwas benutzen zu dürfen* *als ein Dankeschön: „Bitte sehr."*	Here you are. Go ahead. you're welcome / not at all / that's all right

JOKE YOUR WAY round trouble spots

1. "The acoustics in this theatre are fantastic." – "____________________?"
"The acoustics here are fantastic." – "Ah, now I can smell it, too."
2. During the war two German spies[1] were in a pub in London. They didn't want to be recognised[2] as Germans so one of them ordered in English. "Two martinis, ____________________!" – "Dry?" asked the barman. – "No," said the German, "zwei!" The waiter returned, "Two martinis, ____________________, sir."

1 Spione 2 erkennen

20 **blamieren** ist nicht ***to blame***

TEST YOURSELF : Match the numbers with the letters

A. sich blamieren: ______ **B.** jemanden blamieren: ______
C. selbst Schuld sein: ______ **D.** jemanden beschuldigen: ______

1. She *blamed* him for the failure of their marriage.
2. My daughter *showed* me *up* when she beat me at tennis.
3. If you fail the exam you'll only have yourself to *blame*.
4. If at first you don't succeed, try, try and try again. Then give up. No use *making* a damned *fool of yourself*.

TROUBLESHOOT your English

blamieren in der Bedeutung von ...	
sich / jemanden blamieren	show oneself / someone up
sich / jemanden lächerlich machen	make a fool of oneself / someone
blamabel im Sinne von ...	
erniedrigend	humiliating
peinlich, schändlich	disgraceful

- We lost the match three nil. It was a *humiliating* defeat.
- It's *disgraceful* that this town does not have a single decent hotel.

blame: **tadeln, rügen, beschuldigen; Schuld**	
er ist daran schuld / verantwortlich	he is to blame for it
Das hat er sich selbst zuzuschreiben.	He has only himself to blame.
die Schuld auf sich nehmen	bear / take the blame
Ich kann es ihm nicht verübeln.	I cannot blame him for it.

JOKE YOUR WAY round trouble spots

1. "Are you trying to (*lächerlich machen*) me?"
"No, I never interfere with nature."
2. "I wrote that speech myself," the manager announced.
"It's nice of you to (*die Schuld auf sich nehmen*)," his boss said.
3. Fred was shocked by the news that his wife was pregnant[1]. "How could it possibly happen?" he lamented. "I'm always so careful." – "There, there," she consoled[2] him. "Who says (*dass du verantwortlich bist*)?"

21 brauchen – *need, require* oder *take*?

TEST YOURSELF: Right or Wrong?

	R	W
1. How long *did it take* you to write this book?		
2. You *needn't* help me tomorrow.		
3. He *needed* an hour *to* write the letter.		
4. A bank is a place that will lend you money if you can prove that you *needn't* it.		
5. I'd like to give you something you *are requiring*, but I don't know how to wrap up a bathtub[3].		

TROUBLESHOOT your English

1. *Hilfe / Geld brauchen (Umgangssprache)*	need help / money
2. *Unterstützung benötigen (förmlicher als 1.)*	require support
3. *man braucht eine Stunde (Zeit benötigen)*	it takes an hour to do it

1 schwanger 2 trösten 3 Badewanne

The specialist's CORNER

1.	***need*** **als Hilfsverb mit Infinitiv ohne *to*** (*nur* Gegenwart)
	Need we really leave so early? We *needn't* go home yet.
2.	***need*** **als Vollverb mit Infinitiv mit *to*** (*alle* Zeiten)
	Do / Did we really *need to leave* so early? You *didn't need to go* home so early.
3.	***Need something*** **als Vollverb mit Objekt: nur eine Struktur**
	We *don't need* a car in the city. (NICHT: We *need not* a car in the city).

JOKE YOUR WAY round trouble spots

1. It's the final proof[1] of God's omnipotence[2] that he (*braucht nicht*) exist in order to save[3] us.
2. (*Man braucht*) a lot of experience[4] for a girl to kiss like a beginner.
3. To err is human, but to really foul things up (*erfordert*) a computer.
4. How does a man know when he is getting old? – When he (*braucht*) all night to do what he used to do all night.
5. I (*brauchte kein*) diploma to do what I do. Louis Armstrong

1 Beweis 2 Allmacht 3 retten 4 Erfahrung

22 bringen – *bring* oder *take*?

TEST YOURSELF : The choice is yours

1. Tom had an accident. He was __________ to hospital.
2. Tina went to see him and __________ him some flowers.
3. Tom asked her to __________ some letters to the post office for him.
4. A young doctor __________ Tina home in his car.

TROUBLESHOOT your English

zum Sprecher ***her***-bringen	←	**bring**
vom Sprecher ***weg***-bringen	→	**take**

The specialist's CORNER

zu Bett bringen	put to bed
in Ordnung bringen	put in order
im Fernsehen bringen	show on TV
eine Debatte im Radio bringen	broadcast a debate
jemanden dazu bringen, etwas zu tun	make someone do something

JOKE YOUR WAY round trouble spots

1. "Waiter! Waiter! You've (*gebracht*) me a lobster[1] with just one claw[2]!"
   "Sorry, sir, it must have lost its claw in a fight."
   "Okay, then (*bringen Sie*) this one away and (*bringen Sie*) me the winner."
2. "When I was seven years old my father (*brachte*) me to the zoo."
   "Were you accepted[3]?"
3. Soldier: And what happens if the parachute[4] fails to open?
   Sergeant: (*Bringen Sie*) it back and you'll get another.

1 Hummer 2 Schere 3 annehmen 4 Fallschirm

23 **Chef** ist nicht immer ***chief***

TEST YOURSELF : The choice is yours

manager • chef • chief • boss

1. Crazy Horse was a famous ______________ of the Sioux.
2. Our new French ______________ is an excellent cook.
3. The ______________ hates us being late.
4. I'd like to speak to the ______________. I have a complaint to make.

TROUBLESHOOT your English

Küchenchef	chef
Häuptling eines Stammes	chief
Chef, Chefin (Firma)	boss
Geschäftsführer; Abteilungsleiter	manager

The specialist's CORNER

Oberster Bundesrichter	Chief Justice (USA)
Stabschef	Chief of Staff
Staatschef	Chief of State
Chefkonstrukteur	chief designer
Polizeichef	chief of police

- *mein* Chef: *my boss*: Nur vor *boss* können Possessivpronomen stehen.
- In Zusammensetzungen bezeichnet *chief* den höchsten Vorgesetzten einer Abteilung, Einheit oder Institution.
- *chief* als Adjektiv: *most important; main; principal:* Haupt-...
  Smoking is one of the *chief* causes of lung cancer.

JOKE YOUR WAY round trouble spots

1. The receptionist stared at the red-skinned[1] guest and asked, "Do you have a reservation[2], (*Häuptling*)?" The Indian answered, "Sure have, big place near Rio Grande. How!"
2. In the cockpit of a Boeing taking a hundred passengers to their Turkish holiday resort, the (*Erste Pilot*) is celebrating[3] his birthday. After the fourth bottle of whisky he stammers, "I must stop drinking now, I've got my car at the airport."
3. The only reason my (*Chef*) never says an unkind remark[4] about anyone is because he only ever talks about himself.

24 Daten sind nicht immer *dates*

TEST YOURSELF : What is it in German?

1. What's the *date*? ____________
2. Don't forget to *date* your cheque. ____________
3. Young people's clothes *date* quickly nowadays. ____________
4. He's trying to *date* a beauty queen. ____________
5. The *data* is (!) still being analysed. ____________

TROUBLESHOOT your English

a date	*to date*
Verabredung mit Freund(in) Zeitangabe, Datum	ausgehen, sich verabreden (mit) datieren; veralten

eine Verabredung haben mit	have a date with
sich mit einem Mädchen verabreden	to date a girl
Mit wem bist du verabredet?	Who is your date?
einen Scheck datieren	date a cheque

1 rothäutig 2 Buchung / Reservat 3 feiern 4 unfreundliche Bemerkung

The specialist's CORNER

data = wissenschaftliche Daten (Verb in der Einzahl)	
data abuse	*Datenmissbrauch*
data transfer	*Datenübertragung*
data exchange	*Datenaustausch*
***date* = Datum**	
date of birth	*Geburtsdatum*
delivery date	*Liefertermin*
What's the date today?	*Welches Datum haben wir heute?*
best-before / best-by date	*Verfallsdatum*

JOKE YOUR WAY round trouble spots

1. Reliability[1] of (*Liefertermine*) is inversely proportional to the tightness[2] of your company's production schedules[3].
2. Bisexuality immediately doubles your chances for a (*Rendez-vous*) on Saturday night. WOODY ALLEN
3. Which of the boys is older?
   Jock MacGregor, born in Dublin 10. 11. 1996 or
   John W. Wayne, born in Boston 11/10/1996

1 Zuverlässigkeit 2 Enge 3 Produktionspläne

25 **dezent** ist meist nicht ***decent*** und **diskret** nicht immer ***discreet***

TEST YOURSELF : Match the numbers and the letters

A. vorsichtig **B.** geeignet **C.** anständig
D. unauffällig **E.** dezent

1. That was *decent* of him. ______
2. The hospital has no *decent* equipment. ______
3. I like this *discreet* rose perfume you are using. ______
4. We must be very *discreet*. My husband suspects something. ______
5. I saw him glance *discreetly* at his watch. ______

TROUBLESHOOT your English

(in)decent hat etwas mit moralischen Standards zu tun	
ein anständiger Mann	a decent man
ein ordentliches Gehalt	a decent salary
ein wirklich unanständiger Film	a positively indecent film
(in)discreet **hat oft etwas mit Klugheit und Besonnenheit zu tun**	
unauffällig auf die Uhr schauen	look discreetly at one's watch
äußerst vorsichtig sein	be extremely discreet
umsichtig handeln	act with discretion

The specialist's CORNER

- *discreet* kann *diskret* bedeuten: be absolutely *discreet* about an interview
- Verwechseln Sie nicht *discreet* mit *discrete* = einzeln, getrennnt.
  eine Kette unabhängiger Ereignisse: a series of *discrete* events
- Vorsicht ist besser als (Tapferkeit) Nachsicht.
  Discretion is the better part of valour.

JOKE YOUR WAY round trouble spots

Fill in the blanks.

1. It is not the crook[1] in modern business that we fear, but the __________ man who doesn't know what he is doing.
   OWEN D. YOUNG
2. A German businessman entered a Swiss bank. He looked __________ around, went to the reception desk and whispered[2], "I want to invest 300,000 euros." – "You needn't whisper," said the bank clerk, "poverty is nothing to be ashamed of."
3. What is the difference between valour[3] and __________?
   To travel on an ocean liner without tipping[4] would be courage.
   To come back on a different ocean liner would be __________.

26 dick ist nicht immer *thick*

TEST YOURSELF : Right or Wrong?

	R	W
1. He speaks English with a *thick* accent.		
2. Tina takes slimming pills. She thinks she's too *thick*.		
3. I hate reading *fat* books.		
4. Tom's a bit *thick* – but don't tell his parents.		

TROUBLESHOOT your English

thick **ist üblich für Sachen und Körperteile**	
ein dickes Buch	a thick / fat book
dicke Lippen	thick lips

1 Schurke 2 flüstern 3 Tapferkeit 4 Trinkgeld geben

thick **auf die Intelligenz bezogen heißt dumm**	
Er ist dumm wie Bohnenstroh.	He's as thick as two short planks.
***fat / big* = dick für Personen**	
eine dicke / fette Frau *ein dicker / fetter Mann*	a fat lady a fat / big man
freundlichere Ausdrücke für dick	
ein pummeliges Mädchen *eine dralle Dame* *ein beleibter Mann*	a plump girl a buxom lady a stout man

The specialist's CORNER

dick mit Staub bedeckt	thick with dust
dick befreundet sein	be very thick with
Sie sind dicke Freunde.	They're (as) thick as thieves.
mit jemandem durch dick und dünn gehen	stick by someone through thick and thin

JOKE YOUR WAY round trouble spots

Is it thick or fat?

1. There was a boarding house I stayed in where the dust was so __________ on the floor, the cockroaches[1] walked around on stilts[2].
2. The opera is never over until the __________ lady sings.
3. Jimmy is so __________. He phoned his teacher at school yesterday to say he couldn't come to school because he had lost his voice[3].

1 Küchenschabe 2 Stelzen 3 Stimme

27 diskutieren über – Vorsicht Falle!

TEST YOURSELF : Right or Wrong?

		R	W
1.	We discussed about German politics for hours.		
2.	We had a long discussion about German politics.		
3.	I said that politics was not what I wanted to discuss about.		

TROUBLESHOOT your English

Das Problem		
diskutieren über	discuss something	Verb ohne *about*
eine Diskussion über	a discussion about	Substantiv mit *about*

Great minds[1] *discuss ideas;*
average minds *discuss events;*
small minds *discuss people.*

JOKE YOUR WAY round trouble spots

"I want a word with you, Jones," said the boss. "No (*Diskussionen über*) salaries[2] with any other member of staff. It is your own personal business, and you shouldn't go around and (*diskutieren über*) salaries with your colleagues."
"Oh, I wouldn't dream of it, sir," said Jones. "I'm just as ashamed[3] of it as you are."

1 große Geister 2 Gehälter 3 sich schämen

28 eigen = *own* – eine Falle für Deutsche

TEST YOURSELF : Complete the sentences

1.	*Ich sah es mit eigenen Augen.*	I saw it with _________ eyes.
2.	*Ich habe ein eigenes Zimmer.*	I've got _________ room.
3.	*Der eigene Sohn des Chefs war der Dieb.*	_________ son was the thief.

TROUBLESHOOT your English

own **(Adjektiv) kommt in drei Strukturen vor:**	
1. nach Possessivpronomen	He has got *his own* car.
2. nach *of*-Genitiv *mit* Possessivpronomen	He has got a car *of his own*.
3. nach *'s*-Genitiv	It is Tom*'s own* car.

→ MERKE:

- *ein eigenes / das eigene Haus*
  Falsch: ~~an / the own house~~
  Richtig: one's / his / our own house
- Und es gibt noch das Verb *to own*: besitzen.
  We don't own the house, we've rented it.
- Er tat es aus eigenem Antrieb: He did it *on his own*.

The specialist's CORNER

ein Zimmer mit eigenem Bad	a room with a private bath
eine Wohnung mit eigenem Eingang	a flat with a separate entrance
für den eigenen Bedarf	for personal use

JOKE YOUR WAY round trouble spots

Translate the words in brackets.

1. An Englishman was boasting[1] that some of his ancestors[2] had been in the ark[3] with Noah. "At the time of the Flood," replied the Scot, "we the MacNabs, had (*ein eigenes Boot*)."
2. Advert found in a newspaper: Wonderful opportunity[4] for woman to join fishing partners. Must have (*eigenes Boot*) and be able to cook and wash up. Please send photo of boat.
3. If a politician buys votes with private money, he is a dirty crook[5]; but if he buys them with (*des Volkes eigenes Geld*), he's a great liberal.

29 entschuldigen – *apologise, excuse* oder *pardon*?

TEST YOURSELF : Is it *excuse me* or *I apologise*?

1. A young man, seeing a girl he'd like to get to know, says, "________, miss. I'm writing a phone book. May I have your number?"
2. "Officer," said the Sweet Young Thing coming into the police station, "where do I ________ for shooting my husband?"

TROUBLESHOOT your English

Entschuldigung im Voraus für Störung oder Belästigung	Excuse me, is this the bus to Victoria Station?
Entschuldigung nach der Tat	I'm sorry, I'm late.
(förmlich) um Verzeihung bitten	I apologise for being late.
Bitte um Wiederholung bei Nicht-verstehen	(I beg your) pardon? Sorry?

1 prahlen 2 Ahnen 3 Arche 4 Gelegenheit 5 Schurke

The specialist's CORNER

***Entschuldigung* im Sinne von**	
Rechtfertigung	excuse
Abbitte	apology

JOKE YOUR WAY round trouble spots

What is it in English?

1. The new secretary to her boss. "(*Entschuldigen Sie*), is 'comma' written with one or two 'm's?"
2. Manager to his boss: "(*Es tut mir Leid*) that I didn't come to your birthday party. But the day before yesterday, I made a night of it[1], and I had one too many." – "No need (*sich zu entschuldigen*)," replied his boss. "You were there!"
3. "I'm a self-made man." – "We accept your (*Entschuldigung*)."
4. The judge asked, "What possible (*Entschuldigung / Rechtfertigung*) can you have for freeing this defendant[2]?" – A juror[3] said, "Insanity[4], Your Honour."
   The judge, "What?! All twelve of you?"

30 erinnern – *remember* oder *remind*?

TEST YOURSELF : Spot the mistakes and correct them

1. I can't seem to remember your name, and please don't remember me!
2. By the time you reach 75 years of age you've learnt everything. All you have to do is to try and remind it.
3. The trouble with telling a good joke is that it always remembers the other fellow of a bad one.

1 die Nacht durchmachen 2 Angeklagter 3 Schöffe 4 Unzurechnungsfähigkeit

TROUBLESHOOT your English

sich erinnern an	remember something
jemanden an etwas erinnern	remind someone of something

The specialist's CORNER

vorausschauend	zurückblickend
daran denken, etwas zu tun remember *to do* something	*sich erinnern, dass man etwas getan hat* remember *doing* something

JOKE YOUR WAY round trouble spots

Translate the German in brackets.

1. "(*Erinnerst du dich an*) those pills they used to give us in the army to keep our minds off girls?" said one. - "Vaguely," said the other. "Well," said the first. "I think they are beginning to work."
2. You're getting old when the only thing you want for your birthday is not to be (*erinnert*) of it.
3. Son to father: Daddy, (*erinnerst du dich, dass du gesagt hast*) you'd give me £10 for passing my exams? Well, you don't have to pay me now.

31 erst – *first, not … until, not … before* oder **only**[1]?

TEST YOURSELF : Welches *only* bedeutet *erst*?

		erst
1.	How can I believe in God when *only* last week I got my tongue caught[2] in the roller[3] of an electric typewriter? WOODY ALLEN	
2.	It's no fun to go to the airline desk to complain about lost luggage *only* to see that the clerk is wearing your clothes!	
3.	Policeman: Lady, you were doing 85 miles per hour! Lady: Oh, isn't that splendid? And I *only* learned how to drive yesterday!	

TROUBLESHOOT your English

1.	Für ***erst*** als Zeitangabe steht **only** häufig mit Zeitpunkt	
	erst kürzlich erst = nicht vor	I saw him *only* yesterday. They are *only* arriving on Thursday.
2.	Mit ***not … until / not … before***: **nicht vor** betont man den Zeitpunkt	
	Don't leave *until / before* you've finished your work.	
3.	***first*** = **(zu-)erst** betont eine Reihenfolge	
	I'll have to ask my boss *first*.	

1 siehe auch *„zuerst"*, Seite 184 2 meine Zunge verfing sich 3 Walze

JOKE YOUR WAY round trouble spots

Translate the German in brackets.

1. Guide[1] on a tour of Rome: "And this ancient monument dates back over 2500 years." – "That's ridiculous[2]," said one little old lady. "It's (*erst*) 2003 now."
2. A woman lion tamer[3] had the cats under such control they took a lump of sugar[4] from her lips on command. The director came over to Tom and asked him, "Would you like to try?" – "Certainly," said Tom. "But (*erst*) get those crazy lions out of there."
3. "There are two sides to every question," said the new boss at the first meeting, "my side and the wrong side. And (*sagen Sie erst „Ja", wenn*) I've finished."

32 es ist nicht immer *it*

TEST YOURSELF : What is it in English?

1. When I do good my boss never remembers. When I do wrong – (*vergisst er es nie*).
2. (*Es gibt kein*) great genius without some touch of madness[5].
3. (*Es gibt*) lies, damned lies and statistics. WINSTON CHURCHILL
4. Sign in a toilet: Please use the toilet brush. Someone had written beneath: (*Ich habe es versucht*), but now I've gone back to using paper.
5. A pessimist is a man who thinks all women are bad. An optimist (*hofft es*).

1 Fremdenführer 2 lächerlich 3 Löwenbändiger 4 Zuckerstück 5 Wahnsinn

TROUBLESHOOT your English

1.	Beziehen sich ***do, forget, know, tell, try, show*** auf etwas vorher Erwähntes, wird *es / das* nicht übersetzt.
	Er ist krank. Hast du *es / das* nicht gewusst? Didn't you know?
2.	Nach den Verben des *Sagens und Denkens* wie ***say, think, hope*** etc. steht für ***es*** englisches **so** am Satzende.
	Wird er uns helfen? – Ich hoffe *es*. Will he help us? – I hope *so*.
3.	***There is, there are***: kein *es* bei Hinweis auf folgendes Subjekt.
	Es ist kein Kaffee mehr da. *There is* no coffee left.
4.	Bei Bezug auf vorher genannte Personen oder Sachen (im Plural) steht ***he, she, they*** statt *it*.
	Wer ist der Mann? – *Es* ist mein Bruder. Who is that man? – *He*'s my brother. Sind das deine Bücher? – Ja, *es* sind meine. Are these your books? – Yes, *they* are mine.

ABER: Wer hat angerufen? – Es war mein Chef.
Who has called? – It was my boss.

➜ **MERKE:** Wie kommt es, dass ... How come (that)...?

JOKE YOUR WAY round trouble spots

Ergänzen Sie *it* oder *so,* wenn nötig.

1. "Hey Paddy, here's the five dollars I borrowed last week."
"Thanks, Mick. I've got a bad memory for figures."
"Then why the bloody hell didn't you say ________?"
2. Some people can cook but don't do ________. My wife can't cook but does ________.
3. "I hear you went to Europe this year. Which countries did you visit?"
"I don't know ________. My husband bought the tickets."
4. The absent-minded professor's wife went into his study and said, "Do you know ________ was 28 years ago today that you asked me to marry you?" The professor looked up from his work. "And did you ______?"

33 etwas – *some(thing)* oder *any(thing)*?

TEST YOURSELF : Is it *some(thing)* or *any(thing)*?

1. Can you give me ____________ money?
2. Of course, do you want ____________ else?
3. I left ____________ money on the table.
4. Do you need ____________ more money?
5. If I can do ____________ else for you, let me know.
6. There's ____________ interesting on TV tonight.

TROUBLESHOOT your English

some, something, someone **stehen in bejahten Sätzen**	
Ich brauche etwas Geld. *Ich sah etwas Merkwürdiges.*	I need some money. I saw something strange.
any, anything, anyone **in verneinten, fragenden oder bedingenden Sätzen**	
Sonst noch etwas? *So etwas habe ich noch nie gehört.* *Solltest du dich an irgendetwas erinnern, lass es uns wissen.*	Anything else? I've never heard anything like it. If you remember anything at all, please let us know.

The specialist's CORNER

- Auch Sätze mit negativen Ausdrücken wie *nobody, never* etc. sind verneinte Sätze.
  One reason elephants drink so much water is that *nobody* ever offers them *anything* else.
- Rechnet man mit einer positiven Antwort, steht in der Frage *some* statt *any*.
  Would you like *some* milk in your coffee?

JOKE YOUR WAY round trouble spots

1. An intellectual is a man who has found ____________ more interesting than women.
2. A holiday is ____________ you have for two weeks that takes fifty weeks to pay for.
3. "What's all this fuss about plutonium?" said Annette. "How can ____________ named after a Disney character be dangerous?"
4. An expert is a man who is like a eunuch in a harem – he knows all about it but can't do ____________ about it.

34 **Eventuell** ist nicht ***eventual***

TEST YOURSELF : The choice is yours

possible • possibly • eventual • eventually

1. We have made a plan in order to avoid[1] ______________ difficulties.
2. She ______________ passed her driving test.
3. Our ______________ aim is to find a drug against cancer[2].
4. My company may ______________ use your service very often.

TROUBLESHOOT your English

eventual(ly) = **schließlich, letztendlich; Schluss – beschreibt das Ende einer Entwicklung**	
der Gesamtsieger	the eventual winner
Er wurde schließlich krank.	He eventually fell ill.
das End- / Schlussresultat	the eventual outcome
eventuell, möglich (Adjektiv) = **possible**	
eventuelle Risiken eingehen	take possible risks

1 vermeiden 2 Krebs

eventuell (Adverb) = **possibly, perhaps, maybe; may/might** + Verb	
Er kommt eventuell.	He may come.
Ich würde es eventuell wieder tun.	I might do it again.
es wäre vielleicht besser, wenn …	it might be better if …

The specialist's CORNER

schließlich **in der Bedeutung von *immerhin* ist after all**	
Schließlich bist du schon 18.	You are 18 after all.
Er ist immerhin / schließlich dein Chef.	He is your boss after all. / Don't forget he's your boss.

JOKE YOUR WAY round trouble spots

may be • possibly • eventually

1. When I was young, I got separated[1] from my parents in a crowd. I was crying and crying, and __________ I found a policeman who said he would help. I asked him, "Do you think we'll ever be able to find them?" He replied, "__________, but there are so many places to hide."
2. Conscience[2] is the inner voice which warns us that someone __________ looking.
3. He was trying to explain to her about nuclear plants[3] but he wasn't getting through to her. __________ she said: "Yes, but what colour are the petals[4]?"

1 getrennt 2 Gewissen 3 (Atom-)Kraftwerk, Pflanze 4 Blütenblätter

35 fahren – *do, drive, go, ride* oder *travel*?[1]

TEST YOURSELF : Is it A or B?

1. We'd better **A.** *drive with the car* / **B.** *go by car* to Munich.
2. If you want to enjoy the beautiful scenery of Sweden **A.** *go* / **B.** *ride* by train.
3. I love **A.** *riding* / **B.** *driving* on top of double-decker buses.
4. My grandmother has never **A.** *driven* / **B.** *gone* by taxi.

TROUBLESHOOT your English

- ***go to*** : irgendwohin fahren, egal mit welchem Verkehrsmittel
  go to Berlin / to England
- ***go by*** **+ Verkehrsmittel** : Betonung, mit *was* man fährt oder fliegt
  go by car / bus / train / boat / plane (*oder* take the car, etc.)
- ***travel*** : meist bei längeren Strecken im Sinne von *reisen*
  travel through Germany
- ***drive*** **+ Transportmittel** : man ist Fahrer eines Fahrzeugs
  learn how to drive a bus; Please drive carefully!
- ***ride*** **+ Zweiräder und Reittiere** : man ist Lenker oder Reiter
  ride one's bike / a horse
- ***ride*** **+ Verkehrsmittel** : man ist Passagier
  ride on a double-decker bus / on the underground
- ***do*** **+ Geschwindigkeitsangabe**
  We were doing 150 miles per hour.

1 siehe auch „Reise", Seite 132

The specialist's CORNER

an den Straßenrand fahren	pull over to the side
der Bus fährt zweimal am Tag	the bus runs / goes twice a day
erster Klasse fahren	go first class
über einen Fluss (Platz etc.) fahren	cross a river / square

JOKE YOUR WAY round trouble spots

Put in a form of **go • do • ride • drive**

1. Did you hear about the Scot who won a holiday for two in Majorca? He ___________ by himself[1] twice.
2. Policeman: Lady, you were ___________ 85 miles per hour. Lady: Oh, isn't that splendid. I only learned how to ___________ yesterday!
3. One charter flight was so crowded that the pilot ___________ by boat.
4. Chancellor Kohl describing his visit to China: "We ___________ ___________ in one of those rickshaws," he told his wife, "and believe it or not, they have horses that look just like men."

36 falsch – *false* oder *wrong*?

TEST YOURSELF : *false* or *wrong*?

1. Education is the process of throwing _______ pearls before real swine.
2. When you dial the _______ number, you never get a busy signal[2].
3. All good generalizations[3] are _______, including this one.
4. I finally had an orgasm but my doctor told me it was the _______ kind. WOODY ALLEN

1 selbst, allein 2 Besetztzeichen 3 Verallgemeinerungen

TROUBLESHOOT your English

false* = falsch im Sinne von *gefälscht, unecht, unwahr	
falsche Hoffnungen wecken	raise false hopes
unter falschem Namen	under a false name
eine Falschaussage machen	make a false statement
wrong* = falsch im Sinne von *verkehrt, fehlerhaft	
die falsche Nummer wählen	dial the wrong number
auf der falschen Straßenseite fahren	drive on the wrong side of the road

JOKE YOUR WAY round trouble spots

1. An Irishman once led[1] from start to finish in the Olympic Marathon. However, he didn't get a medal because it was a ____________ start.
2. Have you heard about the Scotsman who took his wife's __________ teeth[2] to work with him every day to stop her eating between meals?
3. Today I dialled a _________________ number. The other person said, "Hello?" and I said, "Hello, could I speak to Joey?" He said, "Ugh... I don't think so; he's only two months old." I said, "I'll wait."

1 führen (lead, led, led) 2 Gebiss

37 Fehler – *mistake, fault, defect* oder *error*?

TEST YOURSELF : Right or Wrong?

R W

1. Experience is the name we give our *faults.*
2. Planning means replacing chance by *mistake.*
3. To find out a girl's *faults*, praise[1] her to her girlfriends.
4. A hidden *flaw* will not appear[2] till a machine has passed final inspection.

TROUBLESHOOT your English

mistake	das häufigste Wort für Fehler, die man macht
error	Irrtümer im technischen / menschlichen Bereich
fault	a) betont jemandes Schuld für den Fehler b) ein Materialfehler
defect	ein schwerer Schaden
flaw	ein (versteckter) Materialfehler; ein Charakterfehler
blunder	ein Bock, den man schießt; ein Kunstfehler

JOKE YOUR WAY round trouble spots

1. Fred was shocked by the news of his wife's pregnancy[3]. "It's impossible," he lamented. "I'm always so careful. How could it possibly happen?" – "There, there," she consoled[4] him "who says it was your ____________?"
2. All great discoveries are made by ____________.
3. The only real ____________ are human ____________.
4. All sorts of computer ____________ are turning up now. You would be surprised to know the number of doctors who claim they are treating pregnant[5] men. ISAAC ASIMOV

1 loben 2 auftauchen 3 Schwangerschaft 4 trösten 5 schwanger

38 Frau / Mann sind nicht immer woman / man

TEST YOURSELF : What's the best word for *Frau* and *Mann*?

1. If you think _______ are better qualified than _______ to pick[1] the best candidates, look at who they marry.
2. Every married _______ knows that the most perfect _______ in the world belongs to the _______ next door.
3. A pedestrian[2] is a _______ with two cars, a _______, and a son.

TROUBLESHOOT your English

Frau, Frauen	woman, women
Ehefrau(-en)	wife, wives
eine elegante Dame	an elegant lady
das weibliche Geschlecht	the female sex
Mann, Männer	man, men
Ehemann	husband
ein vornehmer Herr	an elegant gentleman
das männliche Geschlecht	the male sex

The specialist's CORNER

● in einer Rede:	
Meine sehr verehrten Damen und Herren	Ladies and gentlemen
● im Brief:	
Sehr geehrte Damen und Herren	Dear Sir or Madam
● als Anrede:	
Frau / Fräulein Meier	Mrs / Miss Meier
● als Abkürzungen:	
Frau / Herr Miller	Ms / Mr Miller

1 auswählen 2 Fußgänger

JOKE YOUR WAY round trouble spots

male • female • man • lady
woman • wife • husband • gentleman

1. Two business __________ were having lunch one day when two __________ entered the restaurant. "Let's go," said one. "My __________ and my lover have just walked in." – "My God," said the other one, "So have mine."
2. No __________ has ever shot her __________ while he was doing the dishes.
3. A lawyer is addressing a __________ jury, "__________, shall we cast this beautiful young __________ into a dark, dim cell, or shall we return her to her lovely apartment on Park Avenue, telephone 555-0540?"
4. The coach of the Chinese __________ Olympic swimming team goes by the name[1] of Do-Ping.

39 fremd – *alien, foreign* oder *strange*?

TEST YOURSELF : Which word fits best?

alien • foreigner • stranger

1. In some countries __________ are not allowed to own land.
2. Where's the nearest bus stop, please? – Sorry, I'm a __________ here myself.
3. Some people think __________ influences threaten their way of life.
4. The man in front was a complete __________ to him.

1 hört auf den Namen

TROUBLESHOOT your English

fremd in der Bedeutung von ...	
Fremder im eigenen Land sein	be a stranger in one's own country
fremder Staatsangehörigkeit sein	be of foreign nationality, be a foreigner
andersartig, fremdartig sein	be alien; be an alien

The specialist's CORNER

die Fremdenlegion	the Foreign Legion
ein illegaler Ausländer	an illegal alien
Fremdenführer	tourist guide

JOKE YOUR WAY round trouble spots

Find the best solution.

1. The softer the currency[1] in a ______________ country is, the harder the toilet paper. John Fountain
2. Last week we found out that the woman who'd been sitting watching TV with us for the past eight years was a complete ______________. My wife thought she was my mother, and I thought she was hers.
3. My definition of a ______________ is someone who doesn't understand cricket. Anthony Couch

1 Währung

40 **früher** ist meistens ***used to*** – aber Vorsicht!

TEST YOURSELF : What is it in English?

1. Ich wohnte *früher* in der *ehemaligen* DDR (= GDR).
2. Schau, dort ist dein *früherer* Chef.
3. Ich bin der neue Besitzer. Der *frühere* Besitzer ist gestorben.

TROUBLESHOOT your English

1. *früher* + Verb:

***used to* + Infinitiv** drückt Zustände und Gewohnheiten aus, die heute (meist) nicht mehr bestehen, und ist die geläufigste Übersetzung von *früher*.

I used to deal with difficult customers. (Ich hatte früher zu tun mit ...) Das Verb steht im Infinitiv.

- **nicht zu verwechseln mit *be used to doing***
  I'm *used to dealing* with difficult customers.
  Ich bin es gewohnt, mit schwierigen Kunden umzugehen.
  Das Verb steht in der -ing-Form.
- **get used to (*doing*) something**: sich gewöhnen an
  Get used to (driving) a new car: sich an ein neues Auto gewöhnen

2. *früher* + Substantiv:

ehemalig (nicht mehr existent)	*die frühere DDR*	the former GDR
vorherig (Reihenfolge)	*der frühere Besitzer*	the previous owner
früher (zeitlich)	*eine frühere Fassung*	an earlier version

JOKE YOUR WAY round trouble spots

Fill in the gaps using these expressions:

former • previous • used to • used to be

1. Dolly asked Priscilla why she had given up her ________________ boyfriend. "I saw him at the swimming pool one day," she said, "and he looked so different without his wallet[1]."
2. Boss: You look like a shadow of your ________________ self, Tina. Anything wrong with you?
   Tina: I keep seeing white mice[2] every time I try to go to sleep.
   Boss: Have you seen a psychiatrist?
   Tina: No, only white mice.
3. I ________________ suffer from[3] a split personality[4], Doc, but now we're both okay!
4. I ________________ a werewolf, but I'm all right noooooooow!

1 Brieftasche 2 Mäuse 3 leiden unter 4 Persönlichkeitsspaltung

41 ganz – *complete, pretty, quite* oder *whole*?

TEST YOURSELF : The choice is yours

1. She wasn't telling the ______________ truth.
2. This is ______________ a different problem.
3. The film was ______________ good.
4. I felt like a ______________ idiot.

TROUBLESHOOT your English

ganz (als Adjektiv vor Substantiven)

- ***whole, entire*** : ungeteilt, in einem Stück
  He drank the *whole* bottle.
  the *whole* / *entire* world / town
- ***all*** : mit Mengen-, Zeit- oder Ortsangaben
  all morning, *all* day / *all* the time / *all* the way
- ***complete*** : vollständig, kein Einzelteil fehlt; komplett
  the *complete* set of stamps; that's *complete* nonsense

ganz (als Adverb vor Adjektiven und Adverben)

- ***quite*** und ***pretty*** übersetzt man je nach Kontext auch mit *sehr* oder *ziemlich*
  quite good, *quite* right: *ganz* gut, *ganz* richtig
- ***pretty*** wird oft verwendet, um eine negative Aussage abzuschwächen
  pretty cold, *pretty* early: *ganz* schön kalt, *ganz* schön früh
- ***entirely*** / ***all*** wrong: *vollkommen falsch*

JOKE YOUR WAY round trouble spots

Translate the expressions in brackets.

1. You have to get to church (*ganz / ziemlich früh*) to get a seat in the back row[1].
2. Advertising is the art of making (*ganze Lügen*) out of half truths.
3. To me, karate doesn't make sense. You spend (*deine ganze Zeit*) hitting boards[2]. And when was the last time you were attacked by a piece of wood?
4. Thank you for your compliment. I've been collecting compliments (*mein ganzes Leben*). Yours is the third.
5. I said to my son, "Finish up (*dein ganzes*) meat[3] and you'll grow up to be just like Daddy." Since then he has only eaten vegetables.

42 geboren ist nicht immer *born*

TEST YOURSELF : Right or Wrong?

	R	W
1. She is a born Müller (*eine geborene Müller*).		
2. I was born in Berlin (*bin in Berlin geboren*).		
3. He is a born German (*ein gebürtiger Deutscher*).		
4. Tom is a born businessman (*ein geborener Geschäftsmann*).		
5. I have birthday today (*habe Geburtstag*).		

1 letzte Reihe 2 auf Bretter einschlagen 3 Fleisch

TROUBLESHOOT your English

geboren **im wörtlichen Sinn**	
• *Sie ist eine geborene Müller.*	Her maiden name is Müller.
• *Er ist ein gebürtiger Deutscher.*	He's German by birth.
geboren **im übertragenen Sinn**	
• *ein geborenes Genie*	a born genius
• *zu einem Beruf geboren sein*	be born to a job

→ Achtung!

Ich *habe* Geburtstag:	It *is* my birthday.
Ich *bin* in X geboren:	I *was* born in X.

JOKE YOUR WAY round trouble spots

1. "Why do you say George is a (*geborener Chef*)?" – "Because his father owns the business."
2. (*Meine Frau hat morgen Geburtstag*). My present will be a real surprise for her. I'm getting her a toaster. She's expecting a Mercedes.
3. "Why were you (*geboren*) in Dublin?" – "I wanted to be near my mother."

43 gehen ist nicht immer *go*[1]

TEST YOURSELF : What is it in English?

1. *Die Busse nach X gehen stündlich.*	Buses to X ______ every hour.
2. *Das Baby lernt gerade gehen.*	The baby is just learning to ______.
3. *Wie geht's deinem Bruder?*	How ______ your brother?
4. *Deine Uhr geht falsch.*	Your watch ______ wrong.

1 siehe auch „fahren", Seite 58 und 132

TROUBLESHOOT your English

gehen in der Bedeutung von	
sich fortbewegen; fahren; reisen	He *has gone* to London.
Wir müssen zu Fuß gehen.	We have to *walk*.
spazieren gehen; spazieren führen	He likes to *go for* long *walks*.
	They *walk* their dogs every day.

The specialist's CORNER

gehen in übertragener Bedeutung	
mit einem Mädchen gehen	go out with / go steady with a girl
zur Schule / auf die Universität gehen	go to school / university
nicht funktionieren	The plan doesn't work.
es geht nicht, es ist unmöglich	it can't be done, it's impossible, it won't work
Wann geht der nächste Bus?	When is the next bus?
Die Züge nach X gehen stündlich.	Trains to X run every hour.
Worum geht es?	What's the problem?
ans Telefon gehen	answer the phone
Er ist schon gegangen.	He has already left.

JOKE YOUR WAY round trouble spots

Is it *go* or *walk*? Mind the tenses.

1. Father: Why don't you ____________ around the block?
   Son: Why? I'm already here.
2. For every successful man, you'll find somebody who says, "I ____________ to school with him."
3. Modern art: If you can hang it on a wall it is a painting. If you can ____________ around it, it is a sculpture.
4. And there was this good-looking East Friesian who ____________ surf riding. His horse drowned.
5. Sticker on a Mini: This was a Rolls before it ____________ through a car wash.
6. God would never have given us the bicycle if he had wanted us to ____________.

44 **genial** ist nicht ***genial***, ein **Genie** ist kein ***genie***

TEST YOURSELF : There are 2 mistakes. Can you find them?

1. The genie granted him three wishes.
2. That was a genial idea.
3. Tom is an undiscovered genie.
4. Her idea was a stroke of genius.
5. A good genius helped him.

TROUBLESHOOT your English

ein Genie	a genius
genial, erfinderisch	ingenious
genial, glänzend, hervorragend	brilliant
eine geniale Leistung	the work of a genius
ein genialer Einfall	a stroke of genius

→ MERKE:

- Englisch *genial* : freundlich, herzlich
- Englisch *genie* : Geist (in der Flasche / Lampe)
- Englisch *genius* : Schutzgeist (selten)

JOKE YOUR WAY round trouble spots

Where do they fit?

a genius • *an ingenious* • *a brilliant*

1. Student: I've just had ____________ idea.
   Teacher: It's probably beginner's luck.
2. The guy who invented the first wheel[1] was an idiot, but the guy who invented the other three, now he was ____________. SID CAESAR
3. A company is ____________ device[2] for obtaining individual profit without individual responsibility[3]. AMBROSE BIERCE

1 Rad 2 Einrichtung 3 Verantwortung

45 glauben – *think* oder *believe*?

TEST YOURSELF : What is it in English?

1. *Glaubst du, dass sie kommen?* — Do you _________ they'll come?
2. *Ich habe seine Lügen geglaubt.* — I _________ his lies.
3. *Ich glaube kein Wort davon.* — I don't _________ a word of it.
4. *Ich glaube, ich habe etwas gehört.* — I _________ I heard a noise.

TROUBLESHOOT your English

think = meinen, annehmen	
ich glaube schon	I think so
Ich habe geglaubt, er sei Polizist.	I thought he was a policeman.
***believe* = überzeugt sein, für möglich halten**	
Er glaubt (einfach) alles.	He'll believe anything.
Das ist kaum zu glauben.	It's hard to believe.
Ich glaube dir kein Wort.	I don't believe a word (you say).

→ ACHTUNG!

- sein Glaube / er glaubt an Gott — his *belief* in God / he *believes* in God
- sein Glaube an die Politiker — his *faith* in the politicians
- an einen Freund glauben — have *faith* in a friend

The specialist's CORNER

es ist nicht zu glauben	it's incredible / unbelievable
ob du es glaubst oder nicht	believe it or not
sie glauben fest daran	they swear by it
du kannst mir glauben	take my word for it

JOKE YOUR WAY round trouble spots

Is it *think* or *believe*?

1. He ____________ that electricity was invented by Voltaire.
2. Of course I ____________ in luck. How else can you explain the success[1] of people you detest[2]? JEAN COCTEAU
3. Since a politician never ____________ what he says, he is always astonished[3] when others do. CHARLES DE GAULLE
4. An optimist ____________ the glass is half full. The pessimist ____________ it's half empty. The realist knows that before long he'll have to wash the glass.
5. "Do you really ____________ in free love?"
"Have I ever sent you a bill[4]?"

46 gleich – *alike, equal* oder *same*?

TEST YOURSELF : What is it in English?

1. There is (*eine gleiche Zahl*) of boys and girls in the class.
2. My sister and I do not (*gleich aussehen*).
3. I bought the (*gleiche*) car as you.
4. They tried to treat all their children (*gleich*).
5. (*Es ist mir gleich*) what you do.

TROUBLESHOOT your English

equal	*gleich an Zahl, Stellung, Rechten*	fight for *equal* rights
same	*identisch*	we live in the *same* house
alike	*ähnlich im Aussehen*	look *alike*
alike	*gleich in Wort, Tat, Art und Weise*	love friends and enemies *alike*

1 Erfolg 2 verabscheuen 3 erstaunt 4 Rechnung

The specialist's CORNER

Das sieht ihm gleich!	That's just *like* him!
gleich gegenüber	*just* opposite
egal / ganz gleich wann und wo	it *doesn't matter* when or where

JOKE YOUR WAY round trouble spots

alike • equal • same

1. In our company all colleagues are ________ , only the salaries[1] aren't.
2. A woman advertised[2] for a husband. The following day she got fifty replies, all saying the ________ thing: "You can have mine."
3. If I had my life to live over again, I'd start making the ________ mistakes earlier.
4. Wife: It says here that marriage makes people look ________ and I know that I'm beginning to talk like you.
   Husband: Do me a favour[3] and don't talk like a fool.

47 glücklich – *happy* oder *lucky*?

TEST YOURSELF : Right or Wrong?

	R	W
1. You don't look very *happy* today.		
2. I was nearly killed in an accident and I know I'm *happy* to be alive.		
3. We wish her good *happiness* in her new career.		
4. Their children are a constant source of *happiness*.		

1 Gehalt 2 annoncieren 3 einen Gefallen tun

TROUBLESHOOT your English

happiness, be happy beschreiben das Glücksgefühl	
das wahre Glück finden	find true happiness
Sorge dich nicht, sei glücklich!	Don't worry, be happy!
***luck, be lucky*: Glück haben (Zufall oder Schicksal)**	
Das Glück war auf seiner Seite.	Luck was on his side.
Du kannst von Glück sagen.	You can count yourself lucky.

The specialist's CORNER

sein Glück in Amerika versuchen	try one's fortune in America
Viel Glück!	Good luck!
So ein Pech!	Bad luck!

JOKE YOUR WAY round trouble spots

Is it *luck / lucky* or *happiness / happy*?

1. Tom is __________. He has got a wife and a car, and they both work.
2. Best wishes for a __________ and successful[1] first marriage.
3. Amusement is the __________ of those who cannot think.
4. Success[2] is just a matter of __________. Ask a failure[3].

1 erfolgreich 2 Erfolg 3 Versager

48 groß – *big, great* oder *large?*

TEST YOURSELF : Which word fits the context best?

1. Time may be a ___________ healer[1], but it's a lousy beautician[2].
2. If only God would give me a clear sign! Like making a ___________ deposit[3] in my name at a Swiss bank. WOODY ALLEN
3. If your company is _______ enough, your mistakes become standards.

TROUBLESHOOT your English

Zwischen *big, large* und *great* gibt es Überschneidungen. Es ist jedoch ratsam, sich an folgende Daumenregeln zu halten.

- ***big / large*** für Tiere, Orte, Menschen
  Big ist umgangssprachlicher als *large*: They live in a *big / large* house.
- ***large*** beschreibt Maß, Größe oder Anzahl im Unterschied zu *small*
  a large number / amount / quantity of something
- ***great*** beschreibt die Bedeutung einer Sache oder Person
  he's a *great* artist, *Peter the Great*
  Great kann auch vor nicht zählbaren (also mess- oder wägbaren) Substantiven stehen. It gives me *great* pleasure to announce the winner.
- ***tall*** beschreibt Länge, Höhe bzw. Körpergröße
  She's the *tallest* girl in the class. Tom is over six feet *tall*.

The specialist's CORNER

ein großer Verlust	a heavy loss
ein großer Buchstabe	a capital letter
eine große Mehrheit	a great majority
so groß wie ein Fußballfeld	the size of a football pitch
großen Hunger haben	be very hungry

1 Heiler, Arzt 2 Kosmetiker 3 Einzahlung

JOKE YOUR WAY round trouble spots

What is it in English?

1. A small thing can be made (*groß*) by the right kind of advertising.
2. All (*große*) discoveries[1] are made by mistake[2].
3. An American tourist was visiting a zoo in London. In front of the kangaroo house he stopped and exclaimed, "One thing I really grant you Brits. Your grasshoppers are really a lot (*größer*) than ours back in Texas."
4. The giant redwood trees in the USA are so (*groß*) that squirrels[3] have to wear oxygen masks[4] to collect nuts.

49 gut – *good* oder *well*?

TEST YOURSELF : Right or Wrong?

	R	W
1. A good plan today is better than a perfect plan tomorrow.		
2. If you want to eat good in England, eat three breakfasts.		
3. I bet on a good horse today. It took eleven other horses to beat him.		

TROUBLESHOOT your English

good	ist Adjektiv und sagt, „wie etwas ist"	He is a *good* driver.
well	ist Adverb; es bestimmt Verben, Adjektive und Adverbien näher	He drives *well.*

The specialist's CORNER

The wine tastes good.	Der Wein schmeckt gut.
The cake looks good.	Der Kuchen sieht gut aus.
The food smells good.	Das Essen riecht gut.

1 Entdeckungen 2 aus Versehen 3 Eichhörnchen 4 Sauerstoffmaske

- nach *taste*: schmecken, *smell*: riechen, *look*: aussehen und *sound*: klingen steht *good*, wenn eine Eigenschaft oder Qualität beschrieben wird. Man könnte diese Verben durch eine Form von *to be* ersetzen.
- *well* als Adjektiv gebraucht bedeutet auch *gesund, wohlauf.*
  Tina is not well today.

JOKE YOUR WAY round trouble spots

What is it in English?

1. I think if I have a (*gutes*) breakfast I can go without food for the rest of the day. I think that until about lunchtime.
2. One door-to-door salesman does very (*gut*) by using the opening line: "Can I interest you in something your neighbour said you couldn't possibly afford[1]?"
3. Great Caesar's bust[2] is on the shelf[3],
   And I don't feel so (*gut*) myself.

1 sich (etwas) leisten 2 Büste 3 Regal

50 haben = *have* hat's in sich

TEST YOURSELF : Is it A, B or C?

1. Hypochondria is the one disease[1] **A.** *I don't have got* / **B.** *I haven't got* / **C.** *I don't have.*
2. Why do some Germans envy[2] the Chinese? – Because they **A.** *have still got* / **B.** *are still having* / **C.** *still have* their Wall.
3. The telephone will ring when **A.** *you are having* / **B.** *you have got* / **C.** *you've* a shower. You will reach it just in time to hear the click of the caller hanging up.

TROUBLESHOOT your English

have / have got = **haben** in der Bedeutung von *besitzen*	
Variante 1: have something	**Variante 2: have got something**
I *have* a bike. Verkürzung ist nicht möglich	I *have got* / I'*ve got* a bike. Verkürzung ist möglich
Do you *have* a car? No, I *don't have* a car. Frage und Verneinung werden mit *do* umschrieben	*Have* you *got* a car? No, I *haven't got* a car. Frage und Verneinung werden *nicht* mit *do* umschrieben

Verlaufsform ist in keiner Variante möglich.

The specialist's CORNER

Manche Tätigkeiten entsprechen *have* plus Substantiv (Nomen):

frühstücken	have breakfast
duschen	have a shower

Die Verlaufsform (Progressive) steht, wenn die Tätigkeit noch nicht abgeschlossen ist.

We'*re having breakfast* now. We always *have lunch* at 12.

1 Krankheit 2 beneiden

JOKE YOUR WAY round trouble spots

Fill in the correct form of *have* and *have got*.

1. I asked her if she liked Le Corbusier and she replied, "I'd love some – with a little lemon juice in it, if you ______________ any."
2. You can fool 88 % of the public all the time, the rest ______________ any money.
3. There are only two specimens of a Neanderthal's head in existence. The British Museum ______________ one and Bill ______________ the other.

51 halten = *hold, keep* oder *think*?

TEST YOURSELF : Is it *hold* or *keep*?

1. Here's a five dollar bill – please ______________ the change.
2. The police were unable to ______________ back the crowd.
3. Who ______________ the world record for the long jump?
4. We are not allowed to ______________ dogs in our house.

TROUBLESHOOT your English

hold (held, held) **= körperlich (fest)halten**	
Händchen halten	hold hands
stillhalten	hold still
die Menschenmenge zurückhalten	hold back the crowd
keep **= behalten, unterhalten, eine Situation beibehalten**	
warm halten	keep warm
ein Versprechen halten	keep a promise
das Rückgeld behalten	keep the change
sich eine Geliebte halten	keep a mistress

think much of, *believe* in = etwas halten von	
Er hält nichts vom Sparen.	He doesn't believe in saving.
Ich halte nicht viel von ihm.	I don't think much of him.
Wofür halten Sie mich?	Who do you think I am?

The specialist's CORNER

eine Rede halten	make a speech
jemandem die Daumen halten / drücken	keep one's fingers crossed for someone
sich nicht / kaum mehr halten können vor Freude / Zorn etc.	be beside oneself with joy / anger etc.

JOKE YOUR WAY round trouble spots

Fill in the correct verb form.

keep • think • make • hold

1. There are two things that are more difficult than ________ an after-dinner speech: climbing a wall which is leaning towards you and kissing a girl who is leaning away from you. WINSTON CHURCHILL
2. The income tax[1] people are very nice. They're letting me ________ my mother. HENRY YOUNGMAN
3. Sometimes you can make a very effective statement[2] by ________ your tongue.
4. Well, money isn't everything in life, but it does ________ you in touch with your children.
5. "You mustn't pull the cat's tail[3]." – "I' m only ________ it. It's the cat that's pulling."
6. "What do you ________ of our new boss?" – "He dresses smartly." – "Yes, and quickly, too!"

1 Einkommensteuer 2 Erklärung 3 Schwanz

52 **handeln** ist nicht ***to handle***

TEST YOURSELF : What is it?

bargain • deal with • handle • trade in

1. He said he wasn't prepared to ____________ over the price.
2. The company ____________ computer software.
3. A new man was appointed to ____________ the crisis.
4. Her poems often ____________ the subject of death.

TROUBLESHOOT your English

***deal, trade*: mit Waren handeln**	
mit Waffen handeln	deal / trade in arms
mit England Handel treiben	trade with England
***bargain*: handeln, feilschen**	
um den Preis handeln	bargain over the price (with)
ein gutes Geschäft / Schnäppchen	a (good) bargain
***act, take action*: handeln, das heißt aktiv werden**	
sofort handeln	take immediate action
entschlossen handeln	act decisively
***deal with, be about*: handeln von**	
das Gedicht handelt von Liebe	the poem deals with love
das Buch handelt vom Krieg	the book is about war

→ MERKE auch:

mit Menschen / Problemen umgehen können	be able to handle / deal with people / problems
Vorsicht Glas!	Handle with care!

The specialist's CORNER

Worum handelt es sich?	What's it about?
es handelt sich darum, ob ...	the question is whether ...
an der Börse gehandelt werden	be traded on the stock exchange

JOKE YOUR WAY round trouble spots

Replace the nonsense word *woggle*.

1. Men and nations will *woggle* rationally when all other possibilities have been exhausted[1].
2. A *woggle* is something you buy that is cheaper than something you really need.
3. *Woggling* in antiques[2] is a strange way to make a living. It's the only business where grandparents buy something, the parents sell it, and the grandchildren buy it again.

53 Heim- und Hausarbeiten – *homework, housework* oder *outwork*?

TEST YOURSELF : Is it A, B or C?

A. outwork • B. homework • C. housework

1. work that you do to prepare for something ______
2. work for a business that is done by people at home ______
3. work that is given by teachers for students to do at home ______
4. cleaning, making the beds, cooking ______

1 ausgeschöpft 2 Antiquitäten

TROUBLESHOOT your English

Heimarbeit *Heimarbeiter*	outwork outworker
Hausaufgabe(n)	homework
Hausarbeit(en) *Hausfrau, Hausmann*	housework housewife, house-husband

→ ACHTUNG!

outwork, homework, housework

- haben keinen Plural
- werden nicht mit unbestimmten Artikel (*a, an*) gebraucht
- eine einzelne Hausaufgabe: *a piece of homework*

die Hausaufgaben machen:	*do (one's) homework*
die Hausarbeit machen:	*do the housework*

JOKE YOUR WAY round trouble spots

1. Pupil: Would you punish someone for something they didn't do?
   Teacher: Of course not.
   Pupil: Good, because I haven't done my ______________ .
2. "______________ , it's so boring," said the bride. "You make the beds, clean the floors and do the dishes. Then three months later you have to do it all again."
3. He asked her to explain her dreams. "I haven't had any this week, doctor," she said.
   "Well, how the hell can I help you if you don't do your ___________?"

54 hören – *listen* oder *hear*?

TEST YOURSELF : Right or Wrong?

	R	W
1. I like to *hear* classical music.		
2. Although we *listened* carefully, we couldn't *hear* a word of what they were saying.		
3. *Hear!* Somebody is knocking at the door.		
4. We hope to *hear* from you soon.		
5. She was shouting something we couldn't *listen* very well.		

TROUBLESHOOT your English

listen to: (bewusst) **zu-, hinhören, anhören; lauschen**	
Musik hören	listen to music
Radio hören	listen to the radio
auf jemandes Rat hören	listen to someone's advice
Vernunft annehmen	listen to reason
hear: **wahrnehmen, erfahren**	
ein Geräusch hören	hear some noise
ein Gerücht hören	hear a rumour
Ich habe es heute Morgen im Radio gehört.	I heard it on the radio this morning.

→ MERKE:

- Do you listen to the news every morning?
  Handlung ist betont
- Have you heard the news?
  Ergebnis ist betont
- *hear* steht in der Regel nicht in der Verlaufsform

The specialist's CORNER

zufällig mit anhören	overhear
auf den Namen Paul hören	answer to the name of Paul
schwer / schlecht hören	be hard of hearing
Lasst mal von euch hören.	Keep in touch.

JOKE YOUR WAY round trouble spots

hear • listen • listen to

1. If you want your wife to __________, then talk to another woman.
2. "Do you believe that it is possible to communicate with the dead?" – "Yes, I can __________ you distinctly[1]."
3. I __________ you are going into hospital next week for a brain[2] operation – the doctors hope to give you one.
4. There are only two kinds of executives[3] who fail[4]: those who __________ nobody, and those who __________ everybody.

1 deutlich 2 Gehirn 3 leitender Angestellter 4 versagen

55 ja ist meist mehr als *yes*

TEST YOURSELF : Match the numbers and the letters

1. You are coming along, aren't you?
2. Can we trust him?
3. Would you like another drink?
4. Excuse me, sir.

A. Yes, I'd love one.
B. Yes?
C. Yes, of course.
D. Yes, completely.

1. ___ 2. ___ 3. ___ 4. ___

TROUBLESHOOT your English

Das höfliche „Ja" ist im Englischen eine Kurzantwort:	
Kennst du Tom? – Ja.	Do you know Tom? – Yes, I do.
Hast du eine Karte? – Ja.	Have you got a ticket? – Yes, I have.
Können Sie Auto fahren?	Yes, I can.
Angebote und Bitten bejaht man so:	
Some more coffee?	Yes, please.
Would you like to come for lunch?	Yes, I'd love to.
Can you help me?	Yes, of course / certainly.

- Nach einem *Yes* kann man auch mit *but* oder *and* fortfahren.
- Fragendes *Yes*? mit steigender Intonation ist wie im Deutschen eine Aufforderung zu präzisieren, zu ergänzen oder zu erklären:
  Entschuldigen Sie bitte ... – Ja? Excuse me, sir. – Yes...?

The specialist's CORNER

ich glaube, ja	I think so
du kennst ihn ja	you know what he's like
Da bist du ja!	There you are!
Sag's ihm ja nicht!	Don't you tell him!

JOKE YOUR WAY round trouble spots

Ergänzen Sie das *Yes*.

1. "Why, McGregor," said the doctor, "you have lost your stutter!" "Yes, ____________," said McGregor. – "But how?" the doctor wanted to know. – "I've been telephoning Australia recently."
2. Personnel Manager: Can you do shorthand?
   Young secretary: Yes, ____________ it takes me longer.
3. "Did you give your wife a lecture[1] on economy like I told you?" "Yes, ____________." – "And what was the result?"
   "I have to give up smoking."

56 jede(r/s) – *every, each* oder *any*?

TEST YOURSELF : Right or Wrong?

	R	W
1. There are two sides to *each* argument until you take one.		
2. *Each* fool can make a rule[2].		
3. The law protects *everybody* who is able to afford[3] a lawyer.		
4. Did you hear about the Irish millionaire? He ordered two chinchillas for his wife. One for *every* chin[4].		

TROUBLESHOOT your English

***each*: jedes einzelne Element einer begrenzten Anzahl**	
Jede Frage ist 20 Punkte wert. *Und jeder von euch hat eine Frage.*	Each answer is worth 20 points. And you have one question each.

1 Vortrag 2 eine Regel aufstellen 3 sich leisten können 4 Kinn

every: **alle** Elemente einer Gruppe (Größe meist nicht genannt)	
Sie kennt jeden (alle) Schüler der Schule. *Ich konnte jedes Wort / alles hören, das sie sagten.*	She knows every student in the school. I could hear every word they said.
any **= jede(r/s)** beliebige	
Jeder Depp weiß das! *Er wird jeden Moment kommen.*	Any fool knows that! He will be here any moment.

- Für die Substantive *everybody* und *anybody* gelten sinngemäß die gleichen Regeln wie für *every* und *any*.

The specialist's CORNER

mit ***every*** gibt man an, wie häufig etwas geschieht	
die Busse fahren alle 10 Minuten	the buses run every 10 minutes
alle 5 Meilen anhalten	stop every 5 miles
jede dritte Ehe	one in every three marriages

JOKE YOUR WAY round trouble spots

1. He has been invited to ____________ great party in town ... once.
2. A man rushed into a psychiatrist's consulting room[1] saying he thought he had a split personality[2]. "All right," said the psychiatrist. "That'll be five dollars ____________."
3. ____________ club that would accept me as a member, I wouldn't want to join[3]. GROUCHO MARX
4. A bank clerk describes a robber who has robbed the bank four times: "I noticed one thing about him – he seemed to dress better ____________ time."

1 Sprechzimmer 2 gespaltene Persönlichkeit 3 beitreten

57 Karte – *card, map* oder *ticket*?

TEST YOURSELF : Right or Wrong?

	R	W
1. They never taught us how to read a *card* at school.		
2. She sent me a lovely *card* on my birthday.		
3. The documents are in my *map*. But I left it at the office.		
4. Sorry, I can't play *cards* this evening; we've got *cards* for the theatre.		

TROUBLESHOOT your English

Karte	
Fahrkarte, Eintrittskarte	ticket
Landkarte, Straßenkarte	map; road map
Postkarte; Spielkarte	(post)card; (playing) card
→ MERKE: ***a map*** ist keine *Mappe*	
Schulmappe	schoolbag
Aktenmappe, Aktenordner	folder
Aktentasche	briefcase

JOKE YOUR WAY round trouble spots

What's the word for *Karte*?

1. Have you heard about the Irish explorer who paid £10 for a sheet of sandpaper? He thought it was a ____________ of the Sahara Desert.
2. "I hear you went to Europe for your holidays this year. Which countries did you visit?"
"I don't know. My husband bought the ____________."
3. A man on holiday in Italy sent a ____________ to his psychiatrist. It read: "Having a wonderful time. Why?"

58 klein – *little, small, short, minor* oder *tiny*?[1]

TEST YOURSELF : Which word fits best?

1. The floor was covered in (*ganz kleine*) bits of paper.
2. You'll always be Daddy's (*kleines*) girl.
3. There may be some (*kleinere*) changes to our plan.
4. That dress is too (*klein*) for me.
5. He is (*kleiner*) than me.

TROUBLESHOOT your English

small = **klein** (neutral, sachlich)	
ein kleiner Anfangsbuchstabe	a small initial letter
ein kleines Gehalt	a small salary

Gegenteil: *large sums of money*

little = **klein** (gefühlsbetonter als small)	
mit ein klein wenig Glück	with a little bit of luck
Das arme kleine Ding!	The poor little thing!
meine kleine Schwester	my little sister

Gegenteil: *my big brother*

➜ ACHTUNG!

- ***little*** kann nur vor Substantiven gebraucht werden.
  My *little* brother aber: My brother is *small*.
- *little* hat keine Steigerungsformen, deshalb: He is *smaller* than me.

tiny = **sehr klein, winzig**	
nur eine ganz kleine Minderheit	only a tiny minority
ein klitzekleines Häuschen	a tiny little house

1 Siehe auch „groß", Seite 76

minor = klein im Sinne von unbedeutend, geringfügig	
kleinere Änderungen	minor changes
von zweitrangiger Bedeutung	of minor importance
geringfügiger Schaden	minor damage

The specialist's CORNER

von klein auf	from an early age / since I was a child
der kleine Mann	the man in the street
die kleinen Leute	the ordinary people
klein, aber fein	the best things come in small packages

➜ MERKE:

- *small* kann auch *zierlich, schmächtig* bedeuten
- *short* (Gegenteil *tall*) bezieht sich nur auf die Körperlänge. He is *short* and fat.

JOKE YOUR WAY round trouble spots

Small, short or *little* – which fits best?

1. Our farm is so ______________ that the cows have to produce condensed milk.
2. A ______________ girl asked her father, "Daddy, before you married Mommy, who told you how to drive?"
3. The battle[1] seemed lost, so the Italian general gave his last orders. "Listen boys! When the enemy is only 200 metres away you may start retreating[2]. Being a ______________ lame, I'll leave now."
4. Inflation is when wallets[3] are getting bigger and shopping bags ______________.
5. The disadvantage[4] of being the world's ______________ person is that you are the last person to know when it's raining.

1 Schlacht 2 sich zurückziehen 3 Brieftasche 4 Nachteil

59 kochen – *cook, make* oder *boil*?

TEST YOURSELF : Right or Wrong?

	R	W
1. Shall I *cook* you some coffee?		
2. Shall I *boil* or fry[1] the eggs?		
3. The milk has *cooked* over!		
4. I'll *boil* you some soup.		

TROUBLESHOOT your English

- Verwende ***cook*** für das Zubereiten von Speisen allgemein
- Verwende ***make*** für *tea, coffee* oder *soup*
- Verwende ***boil*** für das Sieden bzw. Kochen von Flüssigkeiten oder für das Kochen von Eiern, Kartoffeln oder Reis
- Verwende ***make*** oder ***cook*** für das Zubereiten von Mahlzeiten: make *breakfast, lunch* oder *dinner*

The specialist's CORNER

- Do the cooking: *für das Kochen zuständig sein / es übernehmen*
- He's a good cook: *Er kocht gut.*
- cook the books: *die Bücher / Bilanz frisieren*

JOKE YOUR WAY round trouble spots

Is it *boil, make* or *cook*?

1. The new husband sat down at the table after his young bride had just ______________ her first chicken. "What did you stuff it with?" he asked. – "I didn't stuff it," she said. "It wasn't hollow[2]!"

1 braten 2 hohl

2. The young nurse informed the patient, "Mr Jones, the doctor says you've only got a couple of minutes to live."
"Nurse, is there anything you can do for me?"
"I am sorry, Mr Jones, there isn't much I can do. Well, perhaps I could ______________ you an egg."

60 kontrollieren – *check* oder *control*?

TEST YOURSELF

1. The army used terror to ______________ the people.
2. Our tickets were ______________ twice on the S-Bahn.
3. Please ______________ the oil and water before setting off[1].
4. He was finding it difficult to ______________ his feelings.

TROUBLESHOOT your English

check = **nachschauen, überprüfen, untersuchen**	
Der Beamte überprüfte unsere Pässe.	The official checked our passports.
Würden Sie mal die Reifen nachschauen?	Would you check the tyres for me, please?
Ich glaube, er ist schon gegangen. Ich schau mal nach.	I think he's left. I'll just check.

→ **MERKE:** *ärztliche Untersuchung* = medical check-up

control = **überwachen, unter Kontrolle haben**	
Das Land wird von der Armee kontrolliert.	The country is controlled by the army.
Kontrolle über die Firma haben	control the company
Können Sie nicht Ihre Kinder unter Kontrolle halten?	Can't you control your children?

1 bevor du losfährst

➜ MERKE:

Geburtenkontrolle	birth control
Herr der Lage sein	have the situation under control
außer Kontrolle geraten	get out of control
höhere Gewalt	circumstances beyond our control

JOKE YOUR WAY round trouble spots

1. Old Jake went for his annual (*Kontrolluntersuchung*). "Your hearing is getting worse," said the Doctor. "You will have to cut out drinking, smoking and sex."
   "What?" cried Jake in alarm, "Just so I can hear well?"
2. In my house there's this light switch[1] that doesn't do anything. Every so often I would flick it on and off[2] just to (*überprüfen*). Yesterday, I got a call from a woman in Germany. She said, "Stop it."
3. (*Selbstkontrolle*) is when you go into a supermarket to buy a pint of milk and all you buy is a pint of milk.

61 krank – *sick* oder *ill*?

TEST YOURSELF : Is it A or B?

1. Bad luck! Poor Anne fell ... **A.** *sick* / **B.** *ill* on holiday.
2. Her husband thought she was a very ... **A.** *sick* / **B.** *ill* woman.
3. But I don't think she was seriously ... **A.** *sick* / **B.** *ill*.

1 Schalter 2 ein- und ausschalten

TROUBLESHOOT your English

- ***ill*** steht nur nach Verben, nicht (als Adjektiv) vor Substantiven

fall ill	*krank werden*	He *fell ill* three days ago.
be ill	*krank sein*	He's *been ill* for three days.
feel ill	*sich krank fühlen*	He *has felt ill* since last Tuesday.

- Vor Hauptwörtern steht *sick* statt *ill*. The *sick* child is in bed.
- Sonst bedeutet I'm *sick*: *Mir ist übel.*
  I'm going to be *sick*! *Mir ist / wird schlecht.*

Krankheit	
illness	Leiden; der Zustand, in dem man sich befindet
disease	Krankheit, die (nach Diagnose) einen Namen hat: Alzheimer's disease
sickness	meist Übelkeit: sea sickness, air sickness

The specialist's CORNER

jemanden krankschreiben	give someone a sick note
krank spielen	pretend to be ill

→ ACHTUNG!

Im amerikanischen Englisch werden *sick* und *ill* oft unterschiedslos gebraucht: *Ich bin krank*: I'm sick / ill

JOKE YOUR WAY round trouble spots

1. I'm losing faith[1] in my doctor. All his patients seem to be ________.
2. What does one send to a ________ florist[2]?
3. The art of medicine consists in[3] amusing the patient while Nature cures the ________. VOLTAIRE
4. The personnel manager called John Doorbar into the office and said, "It hasn't escaped me[4] that every time Liverpool is playing at home

1 das Vertrauen verlieren 2 Blumenhändler 3 bestehen aus 4 es ist mir nicht entgangen

mid-week you ask permission[1] to go and visit your grandmother who's seriously ________."

"What an incredible coincidence[2]," exclaimed John. "You don't think, by any chance, she's pretending[3] to be ________?"

62 kurz, kürzlich, vor kurzem – *briefly, lately, recently* oder *shortly*?

TEST YOURSELF : The choice is yours

1. I haven't seen them ____________.
2. She arrived ____________ after us.
3. She met John ____________ on Friday night.
4. I saw him ____________ before he died.
5. We received a letter from him ____________.
6. Tell me ____________ what your story is about.

TROUBLESHOOT your English

kurz; in wenigen Worten	briefly
in Kürze, bald	shortly
kurz danach	shortly after
kurz bevor	shortly before

1 um Erlaubnis bitten 2 Zufall 3 hier: simulieren

The specialist's CORNER

lately / recently – Bedeutungsänderung je nach Tense	
1. mit *Past Tense*	vor kurzem, kürzlich
2. mit *Present Perfect*	in letzter Zeit, seit einiger Zeit

1. "Yes, I *met* Paul at the club *recently / lately*."
2. "I *haven't seen* much of Paul *recently / lately*. Have you?"

JOKE YOUR WAY round trouble spots

What is it in English?

1. "Why, McGregor," said the doctor, "you have lost your stutter[1]!" – "Yes," said McGregor, "I've been telephoning Australia (*in der letzten Zeit*)."
2. Murphy's law: (*Kurz nachdem*) the stewardess has served the coffee, the airplane encounters turbulence[2].
3. Three Scotsmen were visiting London for a holiday and on Sunday they went to church. As the collection plate[3] moved closer and closer, they became more and more worried. (*Kurz bevor*) the plate reached them, one of the Scotsmen fainted[4] and the other two carried him out of the church.
4. Professor: Have you read all of Shakespeare?
   Student: I think so, unless[5] he wrote something (*vor kurzem*).

1 Stottern 2 in Turbulenzen geraten 3 Kollektenteller 4 in Ohnmacht fallen 5 es sei denn

63 lassen – *have, make, let* oder *leave*?

TEST YOURSELF : Right or Wrong?

R W

1. *Let* me answer your question.
2. Why don't you *let* your hair cut?
3. We *leave* the children play in our garden.
4. We *made* him repeat the whole story.
5. *Let* father alone, please. He's very tired.

TROUBLESHOOT your English

let **= lassen** im Sinne von *zulassen*	
jemanden etwas tun lassen	let someone do something allow someone to do something
have something done **= etwas tun lassen**	
veranlassen, dass etwas getan wird *Sie lassen die Küche tapezieren.*	have something done They are having the kitchen decorated.
make someone do something **= jemanden veranlassen, etwas tun**	
Mein Vater ließ uns das Geschirr abwaschen. *Man ließ ihn die Koffer öffnen.*	Father made us do the dishes. They made him open his suitcases.
leave **= lassen**, das heißt den Zustand nicht verändern	
in Ruhe lassen *das Licht brennen lassen* *etwas zurücklassen*	leave someone alone leave the light(s) on leave something behind

The specialist's CORNER

Er ließ den Arzt kommen.	He sent for / called the doctor.
Er ließ mich warten.	He kept me waiting.
Lassen Sie mir Zeit.	Give me time.
Lassen Sie sich Zeit.	Take your time.

JOKE YOUR WAY round trouble spots

Is it *let, have, make* or *leave*?

1. "How was your first day in school, Johnny?"
"Well, I'd hoped for more. I can't read, I can't write, and the teacher won't even _______ me talk."
2. On holiday, people drive thousands of miles just to _______ their picture taken in front of their cars.
3. Anne: Dad, please _______ me take my driving test. I'm old enough now.
Father: You are, but my car isn't.
4. "How was your boat trip yesterday?"
"He not only lied about the size[1] of his yacht. He _______ me row[2]."
5. Advice to bosses: Just _______ the most difficult problems for the laziest[3] managers to solve[4]. They will come up with the quickest solutions.

1 Größe 2 rudern 3 faulsten 4 lösen

64 **Leben** und **leben** – ***life, live*** oder ***be alive***?

TEST YOURSELF : It's going to be difficult

life • live • lives • living • lively • alive

1. Where do you ________? – I'm still ________ at my mother's at the moment.
2. Is your father still ________?
3. My father shows a ________ interest in politics.
4. Don't spend your whole ________ worrying about money.
5. He risked his ________ to save the ________ of his neighbours.

TROUBLESHOOT your English

das Leben	The life [ai] of Brian
die Leben	He saved the lives [ai] of his children.
leben, wohnen	He lives [i] in France.
noch leben, lebendig sein	He is still alive [ai].
lebend (vor Substantiv)	a live [ai] author, a living [i] artist
lebend (nach Substantiv)	the greatest artist alive [ai]

→ ACHTUNG!

- Nur im Verb *to live* spricht man das *i* wie [i].
- In allen anderen Wörtern der Familie spricht man das *i* wie [ai].

The specialist's CORNER

Livesendung	live programme [ai]
lebende Ziele	live targets [ai]
kein lebendes Wesen	not a living soul [i]
quicklebendig sein	be alive and kicking [ai]

JOKE YOUR WAY round trouble spots

Translate the words in brackets.

1. Graffiti: God is not dead, but (*am Leben*) and well and working on a much less ambitious[1] project.
2. Graffiti: Jesus (*lebt*).
   Someone had scribbled beneath:
   Does this mean we won't get an Easter holiday then?
3. The main difference between Los Angeles and yoghurt is that yoghurt has an active (*lebendige*) culture. TOM TAUSSIK
4. "Waiter, there's a dead fly in my soup!"
   "What do you expect for 50p, (*eine lebende*)?"
5. The cardinal rule of politics – never get caught[2] in bed with a (*lebendigen*) man or a dead woman. J. R. EWING (DALLAS)

65 leicht – *easy, light* oder *slight*?

TEST YOURSELF : The choice is yours

1. He didn't make it ____________ for me to leave.
2. I woke up with a ____________ headache.
3. Modern video cameras are ____________ and ____________ to carry.

TROUBLESHOOT your English

***light* = leicht, d.h. von geringem Gewicht; leicht verdaulich**	
Sie ist federleicht.	She is as light as a feather.
Mir ist eine leichte Mahlzeit lieber.	I prefer a light meal.
leichte Musik / Unterhaltung	light music / entertainment

1 ehrgeizig 2 sich erwischen lassen

slight = **leicht**, d.h. klein, geringfügig, nicht gravierend	
ein leichtes Kopfweh	a slight headache
eine leichte Übertreibung	a slight exaggeration
ein kleines Problem	a slight problem
easy = **leicht**, d.h. unkompliziert, schnell, einfach	
Er machte es mir leicht.	He made it easy for me.
Sie ist leicht gekränkt.	She's easily offended.

The specialist's CORNER

Kleinigkeit. / Mit Leichtigkeit.	Easy.
eine leichte / einfache Aufgabe / Erklärung	a simple task / explanation
Nimm's leicht!	Take it easy!
ein leichtes Vergehen	a petty crime
eine leichte Bronchitis	a mild case / touch of bronchitis
Das passiert so leicht nicht wieder.	It's not likely to happen again.

JOKE YOUR WAY round trouble spots

1. He has a (*kleines*) problem with the future. He's getting married in a month and he hasn't found a job for his future wife.
2. It's (*leicht*) to be a humorist when you have the whole government working for you. WILL ROGERS
3. A 70-year-old millionaire had just married a beautiful 20-year-old. "How did you get such a lovely young wife?" asked his friend. "(*Kleinigkeit*)," the millionaire replied. "I told her I was 95."
4. Tim: This letter is too heavy! You have to put more stamps[1] on. Tom: And that will make it (*leichter*)?

1 Briefmarke

66 leihen – *borrow* oder *lend*?

TEST YOURSELF : Tricky translations

1. Kann ich mir dein Auto leihen?
2. Kannst du mir dein Auto leihen?
3. Er lieh sich das Auto von einem Freund.
4. Er lieh mir sein Auto.

TROUBLESHOOT your English

sich borgen, sich ausleihen	borrow something from / of someone
jemandem etwas leihen	lend (lent, lent) something to someone

→ MERKE:

***b**orrow: man **b**ekommt etwas   **l**end : man wird etwas **l**os*

JOKE YOUR WAY round trouble spots

Is it *borrow* or *lend*?

1. A consultant is someone who ______________ your watch to tell you what time it is and then walks away with it.
2. A banker is a fellow who ______________ you his umbrella[1] when the sun is shining and wants it back the minute it begins to rain.
3. Always ______________ money from a pessimist. He doesn't expect to get it back.

1 Schirm

67 letzte / zuletzt – *last* oder *latest*?

TEST YOURSELF : Where do these words fit?

latest • at the latest • last

1. When did you ______________ see Tom Paxton?
2. I saw him when he read from his ______________ novel.
3. He said he'd arrive by 10 o'clock ______________.
4. I wouldn't marry you if you were the ______________ person on earth.

TROUBLESHOOT your English

last = **letztes** Element (einer Reihenfolge)	
Dies ist mein letztes Wort.	This is my last word.
Mach das zuletzt.	Do that last.
Er kommt immer zuletzt.	He's always the last to arrive.
Er kam vorige / letzte Woche an.	He arrived last week.
latest = **neueste, letzte** (im Sinne von aktuell)	
die neueste Mode	the latest fashion
Hast du das Neueste gehört?	Have you heard the latest?

➜ MERKE:

bis spätestens Montag — by Monday at the latest

JOKE YOUR WAY round trouble spots

Translate the German in brackets.

1. The (*neueste*) kind of computer was presented at Cebit in Hannover. Somebody asked it, "What will Germany be like in 2020?" The answer came back in Chinese.
2. "Doctor, I'm afraid I'm going to die."
"Nonsense! That's the (*letzte*) thing you'd do."
3. According to the (*letzten*) statistics, there are three million Americans who aren't working. And there are even more, if you count those with jobs!

68 liegen, legen und lügen – *lie* oder *lay*?

TEST YOURSELF : Right or Wrong?

	R	W
1. He *lay* the money on the table.		
2. Then he *laid* down on the sofa.		
3. He had been *lying* to the police about the money.		
4. His cat was *lieing* fast asleep[1] by the fire.		

TROUBLESHOOT your English

liegen *sich hinlegen*	to lie, **lay**, **lain** / be lying to lie down
legen *Eier legen*	to lay, **laid**, **laid** lay eggs
lügen *jemanden belügen* *Lügen erzählen*	to lie, **lied**, **lied** / be lying lie to someone tell lies

Das Problem entsteht durch Überschneidungen folgender Formen:

- ***lay*** ist Infinitiv von *legen* (**lay**, laid, laid) und
Past Tense von *liegen* (lie, **lay**, lain)
- ***lie*** ist Infinitiv von *liegen* und *lügen,* und beide haben die gleiche *ing*-Form: *(be) lying*

The specialist's CORNER

im Bett liegen müssen	have to stay in bed
es lag viel Schnee	there was a lot of snow
den Tisch decken	lay the table

1 in tiefem Schlaf

JOKE YOUR WAY round trouble spots

1. Cannes is where you (*liegen*) on the beach and look at the stars – or vice versa[1].
2. "Waiter! This egg is bad!" – "Don't blame me[2]. I only (decke) the table."
3. First wife: Does your husband (*liegt*) awake all night?
   Second wife: Yes, and he (*lügt*) in his sleep, too.
4. Here (*liegt*) a poet – where's the great surprise!
   Since all men know, a poet deals in (*Lügen*)[3].

69 lustig – *be fun* oder *be funny*?

TEST YOURSELF : Is it A or B?

1. It's **A.** *no fun* / **B.** *not funny* being a boss. You have to come in early to see who comes in late.
2. It is **A.** *fun* / **B.** *funny* how a wife can spot a blonde hair on a chap's coat, yet miss the garage doors.
3. You're not yourself today. Have **A.** *fun* / **B.** *funny* while you can.
4. Everything is **A.** *fun* / **B.** *funny* as long as it happens to somebody else.
   WILL ROGERS

TROUBLESHOOT your English

be fun	*lustig sein, d.h. Spaß machen, unterhaltsam sein*
be funny	*komisch / ungewöhnlich / eigenartig sein*

→ ACHTUNG!

it's <u>no</u> fun: das ist kein / macht keinen Spaß (*fun* ist Substantiv)
it's <u>not</u> funny: das ist nicht komisch (*funny* ist Adjektiv)

1 und umgekehrt 2 ich bin nicht schuld 3 mit Lügen handeln

funny hat oft eine negative Bedeutung

This tea tastes *funny* (*sonderbar*).
You've got a *funny* way of showing your love (*ungewöhnlich*).

The specialist's CORNER

Die Party war sehr lustig / unterhaltsam.	The party was great fun.
Er ist ein lustiger Typ.	He's good fun.
Amüsier dich gut!	Have fun! / Enjoy yourself!
sich lustig machen über	make fun of

JOKE YOUR WAY round trouble spots

Translate the German in brackets.

1. (*Es ist nicht lustig*) to go to the airline desk to complain[1] about lost luggage only to see the clerk wearing your clothes!
2. She insisted on[2] taking innumerable outfits[3] with her, and they arrived at the airport loaded with luggage. "I wish," said the husband thoughtfully, "we had brought the piano." – "No need to be sarcastic," said the wife, "it's not at all (*komisch*)." – "I'm not trying to (*komisch zu sein*)," he said, "I've left the tickets on the piano."
3. "I didn't come here (*damit man sich über mich lustig macht*)."
"Oh, where do you normally go?"

1 sich beschweren, reklamieren 2 bestehen auf 3 unzählige Klamotten

70 machen – *make* oder *do*?

TEST YOURSELF : What is it in English?

1. *Sie macht ihre eigenen Kleider.* She __________ her own clothes.
2. *Er macht viele Überstunden.* He __________ a lot of overtime.
3. *Ich mache dir eine Tasse Tee.* I'll __________ you a cup of tea.
4. *Tom macht heute sein Examen.* Tom is ________ his exam today.
5. *Ich mache etwa 20 Reisen im Jahr.* I _________ about 20 trips a year.

TROUBLESHOOT your English

do betont die Tätigkeit, das Erledigen einer Aufgabe	
eine Arbeit machen / tun	do a job
Überstunden machen	do overtime
seine Hausaufgaben machen	do one's homework
eine Prüfung machen	do / take an exam
make **betont das Herstellen, die Zubereitung, das Ergebnis**	
Kaffee machen	make coffee
Fehler machen	make mistakes
Fortschritte machen	make progress
ein großes Theater machen	make a great fuss

The specialist's CORNER

Daneben gibt es eine Reihe feststehender Ausdrücke mit ***go*** und ***take***:

ein Foto machen	take a photo
Pause machen	take a break
einen Kurs machen	take a course
Urlaub machen	go on holiday
Urlaub nehmen	take a holiday

JOKE YOUR WAY round trouble spots

do • **hold** • **make** • **take** (Achte auf die Form)

1. I ______________ a speed reading course[1] and read War And Peace in twenty minutes. It's about Russia. WOODY ALLEN
2. In six days God ______________ Heaven and Earth, the Sea and all that is in them – he was self-employed[2].
3. "Waiter! Waiter! What is this fly[3] ______________ in my soup?" – "Hum ... Looks like breaststroke[4], doesn't it?"
4. Honeymoon is the holiday a man ______________ before beginning work under a new boss.
5. Anybody who can still ______________ at seventy what he was ______________ at twenty wasn't ______________ much at twenty.

71 meinen – *mean* oder *think*?

TEST YOURSELF : What is it in English?

1. Have you ever been to a zoo? I (*meine*) as a visitor?
2. If you (*meinen*) nothing is impossible, try getting your name off a mailing list.
3. He's a guy who can say absolutely nothing and (*meinen*) it.

TROUBLESHOOT your English

think = **meinen** im Sinne von glauben, halten von	
Ich glaube das auch.	I think so too.
Was hältst du davon / meinst du dazu?	What do you think about it?

1 Schnelllesekurs 2 selbständig 3 Fliege 4 Brustschwimmen

mean = meinen im Sinne von bedeuten, sagen wollen	
Was bedeutet dieses Wort?	What does this word mean?
Wie meinen Sie das?	How do you mean?
Ich meine, was ich sage.	I mean what I say.
Was hast du dir dabei gedacht?	What did you mean by that?
mean (to) = es ernst meinen, beabsichtigen, wollen	
Ich wollte nicht unhöflich sein.	I didn't mean to be rude.
Ich meine es ernst.	I mean it.

→ ACHTUNG!

- ***opinion***: die Meinung, die man ausdrückt: *express an opinion*
- ***meaning***: die Meinung, die ein Wort, Satz, Gedicht hat:
  Er ist sonderbar, Sie wissen schon, was ich meine.
  He is bizarre, if you get *my meaning.*
- ***meinen*** als Abschluss der direkten Rede:
  Sie sind wohl noch nicht zu Hause, meinte er.
  They won't be home yet, he *said*

JOKE YOUR WAY round trouble spots

Setzen Sie eine Form von *mean* und *think* ein.

1. Just when you ____________ you've got the promotion[1] in the bag, some new guy will come along and marry the boss's daughter.
2. Two psychiatrists passed each other in the corridor. "Good morning," said one.
   "I wonder what he ____________ by that," worried[2] the other.
3. Secretary: Excuse me, sir, I think you're wanted on the phone.
   Boss: What do you ____________ you ____________ I'm wanted on the phone? Either I am or I'm not!
   Secretary: Well, sir, the caller asked if that stupid old idiot was in yet.
4. If God had ____________ us ____________ be homosexuals he would have created Adam and Eric.

1 Beförderung 2 sich besorgt fragen

72 die meisten – *most* oder *the most*?

TEST YOURSELF : Right or Wrong?

	R	W
1. The *most* people in our village are farmers.		
2. The *most* important thing in life is happiness.		
3. The rain in Spain stays *most* in the plains.		
4. It's *most* kind of you to invite me to your party.		

TROUBLESHOOT your English

most **(ohne Artikel) = fast alle, die Mehrheit, der größte Teil**	
Ich gehe fast jeden Tag spazieren. *Er verbrachte die meiste Zeit seines Lebens in Indien.*	I go for a walk most days. He spent most of his life in India.
most **(ohne Artikel) = am meisten, in hohem Maße, höchst**	
Der Film war höchst interessant. *Am meisten fürchte ich einen Krieg.*	The film was most interesting. A war is what I fear most.
the most **= Superlativ, höchster Grad, mehr als alle anderen**	
Paul machte die meisten Fehler von allen Schülern. *Selbstmord ist die ehrlichste Form der Selbstkritik.*	Paul made the most mistakes of all the class. Suicide is the most sincere form of self-criticism.
mostly **= meist(ens), hauptsächlich**	
Wir sind meistens am Abend zu Hause.	We're mostly at home in the evenings.

The specialist's CORNER

das am meisten verkaufte Auto	the best-selling car
das Beste aus etwas machen	make the most of something

JOKE YOUR WAY round trouble spots

most • the most • mostly

1. Selling is ________ exciting thing you can do with your clothes on.
   JOHN FENTON
2. A conservative is a man who thinks and sits, ________ sits.
   WOODROW WILSON
3. Doctor: Say 'Aaaah'.
   Pauline: That's a change! ________ young men want me to say 'yes'.
4. Ronald: Doctor, doctor my hands are trembling[1] all the time.
   Doctor: I think you have got an alcohol problem.
   Ronald: Yes, doctor, I spill[2] ________ of it.

73 Mensch(en) – *human, man, person* (oder *people*)?

TEST YOURSELF : What is it in English?

1. An alcoholic is a (*Mensch*) who drinks more than his doctor.
2. Two (*Menschen*) getting together to write a book is like three people getting together to have a baby. One of them is superfluous[3].
   G. B. SHAW
3. A zoo is a place devised for animals to study the behaviour of (*Menschen*).
4. Our neighbours are nice (*Menschen*). They listen to us attentively[4] – through a wall.

1 zittern 2 verschütten 3 überflüssig 4 aufmerksam

TROUBLESHOOT your English

der Mensch im Gegensatz zum Tier	human, human being
der Mensch als Individuum, Typ, Charakter	person
der Mensch als Gattung	man, mankind
Menschen, Leute, Einwohner, Bevölkerung	people

→ ACHTUNG!

das Volk	the people
die Leute von nebenan	the people next door
die Völker Europas	the peoples of Europe

→ MERKE:

alle Leute everyone / everybody (vermeiden Sie *all people*)

The specialist's CORNER

Ich bin auch nur ein Mensch.	I'm only human.
von Mensch zu Mensch reden	have a heart-to-heart
Was werden die Leute sagen?	What will people say?

JOKE YOUR WAY round trouble spots

The choice is yours.

human being • man • people • person

1. Mother: Helen, what kind of a ______________ is your new friend? Is he respectable?
   Helen: Of course he is, Mum. He doesn't drink or smoke, has a very loyal wife and three well-behaved children.
2. If a politician tries to buy votes[1] with private money, he is a dirty crook; but if he tries to buy them with the ____________'s own money, he's a great liberal.
3. If you want to make a ______________ very angry, tell him you are going to pray for him. EDGAR W. HOWE

1 Stimmen kaufen

4. Doesn't it make you feel a little insecure to know that if you're a ______________, your body is worth 98 cents – and if you're a cow, it's worth $700?

74 müssen – *need, have to* oder *must*[1]?

TEST YOURSELF : What is it in English?

1. "Do you serve women in this bar?" – "No, sir, you (*müssen*) bring your own."
2. If you like laws and sausages[2], you (*dürfen nicht*) watch either of them being made. OTTO VON BISMARCK
3. It's the final proof of God's omnipotence[3] that he (*muss nicht*) exist in order to save us. PETER DE VRIES

TROUBLESHOOT your English

A. müssen

1. ***must***
   der Zwang geht vom Sprecher aus; er spricht aus Überzeugung
2. ***have to***
   a) der Zwang geht von Dritten oder den Umständen aus
   b) *have to* ersetzt *must* beim Bilden von Zeiten: *I had to do it*
3. ***need***:
   dringende Notwendigkeit: *it needs to be done*: es muss getan werden

1 Siehe auch *„brauchen"*, Seite 38 2 Gesetze und Würste 3 Allmacht

B. nicht müssen: Drei Strukturen

Du musst es nicht (tun).

1. You *needn't* do it.
2. You *don't have* to do it.
3. It *doesn't need to* be done.

→ VORSICHT Sprachfalle!

you must not heißt *du darfst nicht*

The specialist's CORNER

Ich müsste ihm eigentlich helfen.	I ought to help him.
Muss das sein?	Is that really necessary?
Das musste ja passieren!	That was bound to happen.

JOKE YOUR WAY round trouble spots

must • have to • mustn't • needn't

1. There are two kinds of men: those we may dream about and those we ____________ marry.
2. I ____________ tell my wife anything. My neighbours do it for me.
3. An Italian prime minister ____________ think of getting married until he gets a steady job[1].
4. Old Jake went for his annual[2] medical check-up. "Your hearing is getting worse," said the doctor. "You will ____________ cut out drinking, smoking and sex."
   "What?" cried Jake in alarm, "Just so I can hear better?"

1 ein sicherer Beruf 2 jährlich

75 Nachricht – *news* oder *message*?

TEST YOURSELF : Right or Wrong ?

	R	W
1. What's the latest *message* about the terrorist attack?		
2. That's an interesting piece of *news*.		
3. Eight o'clock! Can you put the *news* on?		
4. These are bad *news*.		
5. Excuse me, is there a *news* for me?		

TROUBLESHOOT your English

message = **Nachricht**, die man hinterlässt oder überbringt	
Wollen Sie eine Nachricht hinterlassen?	Would you like to leave a message?
Kann ich etwas ausrichten?	Can I take a message?
Irgendwelche Nachrichten für mich?	Any messages for me?
news = **Neuigkeiten, Nachrichten** in den Medien	
Hier sind die Nachrichten.	Here's the news.
Ich habe es in den Nachrichten gehört.	I heard it in the news.
Ich habe eine schlechte Nachricht für Sie.	I've got some bad news for you.

→ VORSICHT Sprachfalle!

- Keine Nachricht ist (eine) gute Nachricht: No news ***is*** good news.
  Das Verb steht im Singular, obwohl *news* ein Plural-**s** hat.
- Vor *news* steht weder unbestimmter Artikel noch Zahlwort.
  Er hat *eine* gute Nachricht für uns: He has (*some*) good news for us.
- Nachrichten zählt man als *pieces* of news oder news *items*.
  The next *news item* comes from Japan.
  These are *two* interesting *pieces of news*.

The specialist's CORNER

jemandem die Nachricht beibringen	break the news to someone
von jemandem Nachricht haben	have news from someone
Was gibt es Neues?	What's the news?
eine Nachricht über Funk	a radio message

JOKE YOUR WAY round trouble spots

What is it in English?

1. "Here's (*eine gute Nachricht*)," announced Radio Eriwan, "Lenin's mother is still alive. Now (*die schlechte Nachricht*): she's pregnant[1]."
2. I think my beeper is a little too powerful. Every time I get (*eine Nachricht*), my garage door opens.
3. My uncle tripped[2] on a broken curb[3] and went to hospital. After examining him, the doctor said, "I have (*eine gute Nachricht*) and (*eine schlechte Nachricht*) for you. First of all, you'll never be able to work again." My uncle said, "Okay, now what's (*die schlechte Nachricht*)?"
4. I climbed a mountain and hollered "Helloooo!" A voice came back that said, "The echo is busy at the moment. Leave (*eine Nachricht*) at the beep, and we'll get back to you as soon as possible."

76 nahe, nächst – *next, near* oder *close*?

TEST YOURSELF : The choice is yours

1. Where's the ______________ toilet?
2. Turn left at the ______________ traffic lights.
3. Tom is a ______________ relative of our headmaster.
4. I'd like to sit ______________ the window.

1 schwanger 2 stolpern 3 Randstein

TROUBLESHOOT your English

***next* = nächste in (zeitlicher / räumlicher) Reihenfolge**	
Wer ist der Nächste?	Who's next?
das nächste Mal	next time
in der nächsten Zeit	in the next few days
***near, nearer, nearest* (örtlich) = nahe, näher, nächst gelegen**	
in der Nähe von London	near London
in der Nähe der Stadt	near the town
der nächstgelegene Supermarkt	the nearest supermarket
***close* = nahe, dicht im übertragenen Sinn**	
ein naher Freund / Verwandter	a close friend / relative
einer Sache am nächsten kommen	come closest to something
der Lösung nahe kommen	come close to the solution

→ VORSICHT Falle!

in der nächsten Zukunft	in the near future
der nächste Weg zu	the quickest way to
in der Nähe	near / not far away / in the area

The specialist's CORNER

von nah und fern	from far and near
Naher Osten	Middle / Near East
jemandem zu nahe treten	tread on someone's toes
aus nächster Entfernung	at close range

JOKE YOUR WAY round trouble spots

1. Once I won a prize for arithmetic. The teacher asked what was 20 multiplied by four. I put up my hand first and said "74." I got the prize for being (*am dichtesten dran*).
2. "How come you were born in Iowa?" – "I wanted to be (*in der Nähe von*) my mother."
3. Asked what his favourite drink was, he replied "the (*nächste*) one."

77 ein paar – *some, a few, a couple* oder *a pair*?

TEST YOURSELF : The choice is yours

1. Lady: Doctor, I keep thinking I'm a *pair of / couple of* curtains[1].
   Doctor: For heaven's sake, woman, pull yourself together.
2. I flew over on Concorde. That plane is so fast it gives you an extra *few / pair / couple* of hours to look for your luggage.
3. Customer: I'm looking for *a few /a pair / a couple* of alligator shoes.
   Salesman: Certainly. What size[2] is your alligator?

TROUBLESHOOT your English

couple für Ehe-, Liebes-, Tanz- und andere Paare	
verheiratete Paare	married couples
pair **für zweiteilige, symmetrische Dinge**	
sich paarweise anstellen *ein Paar Schuhe* *Hose / Schere* *Paarlaufen*	line up in pairs a pair of shoes a pair of trousers / scissors pair skating
***a couple / a few / some* = ein paar, einige**	
Könntest du mir ein paar Euros leihen? *in ein paar Minuten*	Could you lend me a couple of euros? in a couple of / in a few minutes

The specialist's CORNER

vor ein paar Tagen *alle paar Minuten*	the other day every few minutes

1 Vorhang 2 Größe

JOKE YOUR WAY round trouble spots

Fill in the missing words.

1. An Irish businessman went to see his doctor about his sexual problems. "You've been working too hard. Get some exercise[1]," the doctor advised. "Try riding a bike ________________ miles every day." Four days later, the doctor received a telephone call from the man. "How are you this morning? Has your sex life improved[2]?" he asked. "How would I know? I'm seventy miles from home," was the angry reply.
2. Lady at the store: I am a physical education teacher and I would like to buy ________________ of shorts to wear around my gymnasium[3]. Sales assistant: Well, how big is your gymnasium?
3. At a party ________________ was discussing the difficulties of family budgets[4]. "I really don't want a lot of money," said the girl. "I just wish we could afford[5] to live the way we're living now."

78 passen – *fit, go with, match* oder *suit*?

TEST YOURSELF : Right or Wrong?

	R	W
1. I work part time, which *fits* me fine.		
2. He *suits* the description of the bank robber.		
3. The book is small enough to *fit* in your pocket.		

1 körperliche Betätigung 2 verbessert 3 Turnhalle 4 Haushaltsgeld 5 sich leisten

TROUBLESHOOT your English

fit = **passen** (der Größe, Form etc. nach, gut sitzen)	
Die Schuhe passen perfekt.	The shoes fit perfectly.
Der Schlüssel passt nicht ins Schloss.	The key doesn't fit the lock.
Tom passt nicht in unsere Kreise.	Tom doesn't fit in our circles.
Passen die Kinder auf den Rücksitz?	Will the kids fit in the back of the car?
suit = **genehm sein; jemandem stehen, passen**	
Montag passt mir gut.	Monday suits me fine.
Blau steht dir.	Blue suits you.
match = **zueinander passen** (in Stil, Farbe, Charakter)	
ein Schal und passende Handschuhe	a scarf with gloves to match
Tom und Tina passen gut zueinander.	Tom and Tina are a good match / suit each other.
go with = **passen zu, harmonieren mit** (für Dinge)	
Die Jacke passt nicht zum Hemd.	The jacket doesn't go with the shirt.
Welche Schuhe passen am besten zu diesem Kleid?	Which of the shoes go best with this dress?

The specialist's CORNER

Das passt überhaupt nicht zu ihm.	That's not like him at all.
Die Bemerkung passt hier nicht.	That remark is out of place here.
Das könnte dir so passen!	You'd like that, wouldn't you?

JOKE YOUR WAY round trouble spots

1. She's got a memory like an elephant and a shape[1] to ________.
2. Bob: I really like your suit. It ________ you like a glove.
   Ron: That's the trouble. It should ________ me like a suit.
3. The tall blonde told the assistant in the fashion[2] shop that she wanted a pair of low heels[3].
   "To ________ what, madam?"
   "A short, plump, rich millionaire," she replied.

79 Pause – *break, pause* oder *rest*?

TEST YOURSELF : Which word fits best?

break • pause • recess • rest

1. We decided to take a short ________.
2. At school kids have ________ in Britain or ________ in the USA.
3. After a ________, she said 'Yes.'
4. I've got a headache. Can we stop for a minute? I need a ________.

TROUBLESHOOT your English

pause	*Denk-, Atempause*	pause for breath / thought
break	*Mittags-, Kaffeepause*	lunch break, coffee break
	Schulpause	break (USA: recess)
rest	*Verschnauf-, Ruhepause*	
	sich ausruhen	take a rest

You have to take a *rest* from all your hard work.

1 Form, Gestalt 2 Mode 3 Schuhe mit niedrigen Absätzen

interval	*Theater-, Konzertpause* (USA: intermission) We had a quick drink in the interval.
recess	*Parlamentspause; Schulpause (USA)*

JOKE YOUR WAY round trouble spots

1. "You're late," said the boss to his secretary when she strolled in at 10 a.m. "I'm not really late, sir," she said. "I just took my (*Kaffeepause*) before I came in."
2. God created the world in six days. On the seventh day, He had a (*Ruhepause*). On the eighth day, He started getting complaints[1].

80 Pension – *pension, retirement* oder *rent*?

TEST YOURSELF : Fill in the blanks

1. At the ________________ I stayed in, they changed the sheets[2] every week. From one room to another.
2. Tom has to live on a small ________________.
3. We all wish you a long and happy ________________.

TROUBLESHOOT your English

***retirement* = Ruhestand**	
in Pension gehen	retire
in den Ruhestand versetzen	pension off / retire someone
vorgezogener Ruhestand	early retirement

1 Reklamation, Beschwerde 2 Bettlaken

pension = **Ruhegehalt**	
von einer kleinen Rente leben	live on a small pension
Pensionskasse	pension fund
Versorgungsplan	pension scheme
boarding house = **Pension, kleines Familienhotel**	
Pension	boarding house / guest house
Vollpension, Halbpension	full board, half board

→ ACHTUNG! ***rent*** ist nicht die Rente, sondern die Miete
pay rent: *Miete zahlen*

JOKE YOUR WAY round trouble spots

1. Have you noticed how every prominent politician, even former[1] prime ministers, decide[2] to write books when they (*in Pension gehen*)? It would have been better for the country if they had read one.
2. Misunderstanding in a clothes shop: "I need some underpants[3]." – "How long do you want them?" – "I want to buy them, not to (*mieten*) them."

81 Platz – *place, room, space* oder *seat*?

TEST YOURSELF : What is it in English?

1. Bitte nehmen Sie neben mir Platz.
2. Machen Sie Platz für den Präsidenten und seine Frau.
3. Ich hätte gerne einen Fensterplatz.
4. Ist genug Platz für meinen Koffer?

1 früher, ehemalig 2 beschließen 3 Unterhosen

TROUBLESHOOT your English

place **= Ort, Stelle**, wo etwas hingehört	
Dein Platz ist bei deiner Firma.	Your place is with your company.
Alle Ordner sind an ihrem Platz.	All the files are in their proper place.
space **= begrenzter Platz**, den Menschen und Dinge brauchen	
viel Platz benötigen	require a lot of space
aus Platzgründen	for space reasons
Parkraum, Parkplatz	parking space
seat **= Sitzplatz**	
jemandem seinen Platz anbieten	offer someone one's seat
Nehmen Sie doch Platz!	Have a seat!
room **= Spielraum, Bewegungsfreiheit**	
Es ist noch viel Platz.	There's plenty of room left.
Platz machen	make room

→ VORSICHT!

stattfinden: take place

Raumschiff: spaceship

Platz nehmen: take a chair / sit down

Raumfähre: space shuttle

JOKE YOUR WAY round trouble spots

place • seat • space • room

1. The __________ between her breasts[1] was called Silicon Valley.
2. You have to get to church pretty early to get a __________ in the back row.
3. God isn't dead; he just couldn't find a parking __________.
4. He heard that most accidents take __________ within five miles of the home, so he moved[2].
5. Wife: Did you notice how the opera singer's voice filled the hall?
   Husband: Yes. I also noticed that a lot of people left to make __________ for it.

1 Brüste 2 umziehen

82 Politik – *politics* oder *policy*?

TEST YOURSELF : Right or Wrong?

	R	W
1. Let's not talk about *politics* now.		
2. What is the party's *politics* on immigration?		
3. Honesty is the best *politic*.		
4. Read your *policy* very carefully before you sign it.		

TROUBLESHOOT your English

politics (nur pl.) = **polit. Einstellung, Betätigung, Wissenschaft**	
in die Politik eintreten	go into politics
Wie ist seine politische Einstellung?	What are his politics?
policy = **Politik** als Strategie, Taktik, Kurs, Linie	
Politik der Härte	hard-line policy
Wirtschaftspolitik	economic policy
die Absatzstrategie (einer Firma)	the marketing policy

The specialist's CORNER

Versicherungspolice	insurance policy
Machtpolitiker / Machtpolitik	power politician / power politics

JOKE YOUR WAY round trouble spots

policy • politician • politics

1. A ___________ is a person with whose ___________ we don't agree. If we agree with him, he is a statesman.
2. Mrs Smith had two grown-up sons. One went into ___________ and the other is a nice, hard-working boy.

3. An insurance salesman[1] was trying to sell a __________ to a factory owner. "I've got all the insurance I need," said the businessman. "Fire, accident, life – the lot. So don't waste your time." "Are you covered against floods[2]?" asked the salesman. "Floods?" said the businessman with interest. "How do you arrange a flood?"

83 Preis – *price* oder *prize*?

TEST YOURSELF : Right or Wrong?

	R	W
1. It's terrible bringing up a family today, considering[3] the *price* of beer and cigarettes. WOODY ALLEN		
2. I really don't deserve[4] this *price*. But then, I've got arthritis and I didn't deserve that either.		
3. If there is ever a *prize* on your head take it.		

TROUBLESHOOT your English

der Preis, den man bezahlt	**price [s]**
der Preis, den man gewinnt	**prize [z]; award**
Alles hat seinen Preis.	There's a price to pay for everything.
Er bekam nur den zweiten Preis.	He only got second prize.

JOKE YOUR WAY round trouble spots

Is it *price* or *prize*?

1. How do you double the __________ of a Trabi? – Fill up the petrol tank.
2. Steve has been awarded[5] first __________ for the best salesman of the year. He sold two milking machines to a farmer with one cow, and took the cow as a down payment[6].

1 Versicherungskaufmann 2 Überschwemmung 3 in Anbetracht 4 verdienen 5 verliehen bekommen 6 Anzahlung

84 Profit / profitieren – *profit* oder *benefit*?

TEST YOURSELF : What is it in English?

1. An accountant[1] is a man whom we hire to explain to the tax authorities that we haven't made the (*Profit*) they think we have.
2. There isn't much (*Profit*) in running a restaurant these days.
3. The new sports centre will bring lasting (*Gewinn*) to the community.

TROUBLESHOOT your English

profit(s): der finanzielle Gewinn im Gegensatz zu Verlust	***benefit***: der ideelle Gewinn, **Vorteil, Nutzen aus einer Situation**
The company made a healthy *profit* last year.	I've had the *benefit* of a good education.

JOKE YOUR WAY round trouble spots

Is it *profit(s)* or *benefit*?

1. It's a socialist idea that making ____________ is a vice[2]; I consider the real vice is making losses[3]. WINSTON CHURCHILL
2. How to be insulting[4]: I wish I had a lower IQ, so I could ____________ from your conversation.
3. Journalist: How can you make money selling cars so cheaply?
   Manager: No problem. We ____________ from repairing them.

1 Buchhalter 2 Laster 3 Verluste 4 beleidigend

85 Prozess – *process, court case* oder *trial*?

TEST YOURSELF : What is it in English?

1. Reforming the education system will be a slow (*Prozess*).
2. He won the (*Prozess*) against his doctor and was awarded damages[1].
3. She is awaiting (*einen Prozess*) on corruption charges.

TROUBLESHOOT your English

process = **Prozess** im Sinne von Vorgang, Verfahren(sweise)	
Lernprozess	learning process
Herstellungsverfahren	manufacturing process
process = **Prozess** in der Bedeutung von Gerichtsverfahren	
einen Prozess gegen ... anstrengen	bring an action against ...
einen Prozess gewinnen / verlieren	win / lose a case
einen fairen (Straf-)Prozess bekommen	receive a fair trial

The specialist's CORNER

- ***court*** das Gericht, vor das man kommt
- ***case*** Fall, Rechtsstreit, den man verlieren kann
- ***action*** Zivilprozess; Klage, die man anstrengt
- ***proceedings*** das Verfahren, die Verhandlung vor Gericht
- ***trial*** Strafprozess, den man gemacht bekommt

Ich werde Sie verklagen.	I'll take you to court.
Der Richter eröffnete das Verfahren.	The judge opened court.
kurzen Prozess machen mit ...	make short work of ...

1 Schadensersatz zugesprochen bekommen

JOKE YOUR WAY round trouble spots

case • court • process • trial

1. McTavish was accused[1] of having embezzled[2] a large sum of money. "Not guilty," said the judge after a lengthy ____________.
"Does that mean I can keep the money?" asked McTavish.
2. "In __________" means that somebody's working on it somewhere.
3. A man was taken to ____________ for speeding[3] and went before the judge. "What will you take, 30 days or £30?" said the judge. "I think I'll take the money," the man replied.
4. My lawyer is beyond brilliant. In a recent ____________, he told his client, "Don't worry. The judge is my cousin. Their witness[4] goes with my secretary. And I'm planning to bribe[5] four of the jurors. Meanwhile[6], try to escape!"

1 angeklagt 2 veruntreuen 3 Geschwindigkeitsüberschreitung 4 Zeuge 5 bestechen
6 in der Zwischenzeit

86 Reise – *journey, voyage, travel, trip* oder *tour*[1]?

TEST YOURSELF : Right or Wrong?

		R	W
1.	Who wrote Gulliver's *Travels*?		
2.	I booked a *journey* on the Queen Mary.		
3.	We went on a day *trip* to the mountains.		
4.	The Titanic sank on its first *voyage.*		
5.	They went on a long train *trip* across India.		
6.	I am *travelling* to Italy on Monday.		

TROUBLESHOOT your English

größere Landreise	a journey across Siberia
Seereise (Weltraumflug)	a voyage to Australia
Kreuzfahrt in die Karibik	a cruise to the Caribbean
größere Rundreise	a tour of Italy
kurzer Ausflug; Urlaubsreise	a trip to Oxford
Geschäftsreise	go on a business trip
Gullivers Reisen	Gulliver's Travels

The specialist's CORNER

mit dem Zug / Flugzeug reisen	travel by train / air
ins Ausland reisen	travel abroad
nach Italien reisen	go to Italy

→ ACHTUNG!

- ***to travel*** betont das Transportmittel oder die Aktivität
- ***to go to*** nehme man, wenn man an das Reiseziel denkt

1 Siehe auch *„fahren"*, Seite 58

JOKE YOUR WAY round trouble spots

tour • trip • voyage

1. A guide on a conducted[1] ____________ of Italy: "And this ancient monument dates back over 2500 years." – "Don't be ridiculous[2]," said one little old lady. "It's only 2003 now."
2. I took a weekend ____________ to Istanbul last week. One chap sitting in the plane was trembling and biting his nails. He had turned bright green. It worried me a bit – he was the pilot.
3. A journalist asked Sir Winston Churchill why he thought he had lived so long. "Well, I'm convinced[3] that it's the whisky and the cigars." "Nothing else?" the journalist wanted to know. "Just one more thing – cancelling my ____________ on the Titanic."

87 Rezept – *prescription, recipe, receipt* oder *reception*?

TEST YOURSELF : Right or Wrong?

	R	W
1. The doctor gave me a *reception* for antibiotics.		
2. What's her *recipe* for success?		
3. There's no *prescription* for happiness.		
4. His latest book met with a mixed *receipt.*		

1 geführt, mit Führung 2 albern 3 überzeugt

TROUBLESHOOT your English

***prescription*: das Rezept von einem Arzt**	
Rezeptgebühren	prescription charges
nur auf Rezept erhältlich	available on prescription
rezeptpflichtig	prescription-only
etwas verschreiben	prescribe something
***recipe*: das Rezept aus dem Kochbuch**	
ein Rezept für einen Apfelkuchen	a recipe for apple pie
Kochbuch	recipe book; cookbook

→ ACHTUNG!

- ***receipt***: Quittung (für eine bezahlte Rechnung)
- ***reception***: Empfang (im Hotel, anlässlich eines Ereignisses)

The specialist's CORNER

Rezept im Sinne von *Heilmittel*	cure, remedy
Das beste Rezept für dich ist Ruhe.	The best cure for you is rest.
Es gibt kein einfaches Rezept gegen Arbeitslosigkeit.	There is no simple remedy for unemployment.

JOKE YOUR WAY round trouble spots

prescription • reception • receipt • recipe

1. Opening line for public speakers[1]: After such a warm ______________ I can hardly wait to hear myself speak.
2. A ______________ in a Scottish cookbook: First, you borrow[2] a pot...
3. "I'll give you a ______________ for some sleeping pills," says the doctor. "They will last for four weeks." – "Oh, thank you, doctor, but I didn't want to sleep so long," answers the lady.

1 Redner 2 sich ausleihen

4. The director was looking over the expense accounts[1] of the sales department. "What are these ____________ here?" he asked his sales manager. "They seem a bit excessive." – "Oh, those are our restaurant bills." – "Well, in future," said the director, "don't buy any more restaurants."

88 richtig – *correct, proper(ly), real* oder *right*?

TEST YOURSELF : Which is the best word for *richtig*?

1. Is that a ____________ diamond?
2. I hope we're doing the ____________ thing.
3. What a mess! You should do your homework ____________.
4. If my calculations are ____________, we should arrive in 15 minutes.

TROUBLESHOOT your English

***right* = richtig**, d.h. recht, genau	
Das finde ich nicht richtig.	I don't think it's right.
Geht deine Uhr richtig?	Is your watch right?
***real* = richtig**, d.h. wirklich, echt	
ein richtiger Engländer	a real (true) Englishman
seine richtige Mutter	his real mother
***correct* = richtig**, d.h. fehlerfrei, genau	
die richtige Aussprache	the correct pronunciation
Ist das die richtige Antwort?	Is that the correct answer?
Hast du genaue Uhrzeit?	Do you have the correct time?
***proper(ly)* = richtig**, d.h. passend, angemessen, ordentlich	
Es funktioniert nicht richtig.	It isn't working properly.
Mach es richtig!	Do it properly!

1 Spesenkonten

The specialist's CORNER

So ist's richtig!	That's the idea!
Bob ist genau der richtige Mann.	Bob's just the man we need.
Ich fand ihn richtig nett.	I thought he was really nice.
Ich hatte drei Richtige im Lotto.	I got three right in the lotto.

JOKE YOUR WAY round trouble spots

What is it in English?

1. My birthday gift to my wife will be a (*richtige*) surprise for her. I'm getting her a toaster. She's expecting a Mercedes.
2. You know your house isn't (*richtig*) insulated[1] when you have to put snow tires[2] on your vacuum cleaner[3].
3. French politicians say, "We want Britain to take her (*richtigen*) place in Europe," and they mean, "somewhere behind Albania or Bulgaria."
4. An ex-president was asked whether he thought it was (*richtig*) for a man of his seventy-five years to be president. The ex-president answered, "In this country, that's about the only job an old man can get."

89

ruhig – *calm, quiet, silent* oder *still*?

1. I was looking forward to a ________ holiday by the sea.
2. We found a ________ town where time seemed to stand ________.
3. The sea was ________ when we arrived there.
4. A group of ________ onlookers was watching our arrival.

1 isoliert 2 Winterreifen 3 Staubsauger

TROUBLESHOOT your English

quiet(ly) **= schweigsam; geruhsam, leise;** Gegenteil von laut	
Sei ruhig / halt den Mund!	Be quiet! / Keep quiet!
Elektroautos sind leise.	Electric cars are quiet.
calm(ly) **= ruhig und gelassen;** nicht aufgeregt	
in ruhigem Ton	in a calm voice
die Ruhe bewahren	keep calm / remain calm
silent(ly) **= schweigend;** Gegenteil von sprechend; lautlos	
Stummfilm	silent film
Sie betete schweigend.	She prayed silently.
die schweigende Mehrheit	the silent majority
still (Adjektiv) **= ruhig, bewegungslos**	
Kannst du nicht still sitzen?	Can't you sit still?
ein Stillleben	a still life
Stille Wasser sind tief.	Still waters run deep.

➜ MERKE!

- Zwischen *silent* und *quiet* gibt es Überlappungen:
  She crept *silently / quietly* out of the room.
  The car rolled *silently* downhill. He's the strong, *silent / quiet* type.
- *still* als Adverb = noch (immer).
  He's pretty old. When he was young, the Dead Sea was *still* alive.

The specialist's CORNER

sich beruhigen	to calm / quieten down
Ich habe keine ruhige Minute.	I don't get a moment's peace / rest.
Du kannst ruhig dableiben.	You can stay if you want.
Das können Sie ruhig tun.	Feel free to do so.

JOKE YOUR WAY round trouble spots

What is it in English?

1. "This car," said the salesman, "runs so (*ruhig*) you can't hear it, so perfectly you can't smell it and so fast you can't see it." Fred considered this for a moment. "Then how the hell do we know it's there?"
2. In the supermarket a gentleman was pushing a pram with a screaming boy. He tried to (*ihn beruhigen*) repeating phrases like, "Don't get excited, Albert. Albert, don't yell! Do keep (*ruhig*), Albert." A woman standing next to him said, "It's fantastic how you look after little Albert." The man turned round and said (*ruhig*), "Madam, I am Albert."

90 Sache – *cause, matter, point* oder *thing*?

TEST YOURSELF : What is it in English?

1. Pack your (*Sachen*) for the trip tomorrow.
2. He gave all his money to a humanitarian (*Sache*).
3. It's a private (*Sache*).
4. I'll come straight to the (*Sache*): we need more money.

TROUBLESHOOT your English

things = **Dinge, Sachen**, die einem gehören	
seine Sachen im Büro vergessen	leave one's things at the office
Er hatte andere Sachen im Kopf.	He had his mind on other things.
matter = **Sache** in der Bedeutung von **Angelegenheit, Frage**	
Was ist Sache / los?	What is the matter?
Ansichtssache	a matter of opinion
eine Frage von Leben oder Tod	a matter of life and death
point = **Sache** in der Bedeutung von **Thema, Punkt**	
Kommen wir zur Sache!	Let's come to the point!
Bleiben Sie beim Thema!	Keep to the point!
cause = **Sache** in der Bedeutung von (gute) **Sache, Anliegen**	
für eine gute Sache kämpfen	fight for a good cause
gemeinsame Sache machen mit ...	make common cause with ...

The specialist's CORNER

Das ist Sache der Polizei.	That's the business of the police.
Kümmere dich um deine eigenen Sachen!	Mind your own business!
eine Ehrensache	an affair of honour

JOKE YOUR WAY round trouble spots

cause • matter • point • things

1. Whenever the ___________ of the people is entrusted[1] to professors, it is lost. NIKOLAI LENIN
2. Success is just a ___________ of luck. Ask a failure[2]. EARL WILSON
3. I have come to the conclusion that politics is too serious a ___________ to be left to the politicians. CHARLES DE GAULLE
4. Englishmen hate two ___________: racial discrimination and Irishmen.
5. Only when the final draft[3] of the document has been typed up and printed will the boss remember some important ___________ that must be added to the middle of it.

91 sagen – *say* oder *tell*?

TEST YOURSELF : Right or Wrong?

	R	W
1. Tact is thinking all you *say* without *telling* all you think.		
2. Some people have tact and others *say* the truth.		
3. A diplomat is a man who can *tell* you to go to hell in such a way that you actually look forward to[4] the trip.		

TROUBLESHOOT your English

***say* = sagen** leitet die Rede ein oder schließt sie ab	
Sie sagte, sie sei krank.	She said (that) she was ill.
„Was für ein Unsinn", sagte er.	"What nonsense," he said.
Das ist genau das, was ich sagte.	That's exactly what I said.

1 anvertrauen 2 Versager 3 Entwurf 4 sich freuen auf

tell = **mitteilen, anordnen** mit direktem Personenobjekt	
jemandem etwas sagen	tell somebody something
jemandem sagen, was er tun soll	tell somebody what to do
***tell* = erzählen, sagen mit abstraktem Objekt**	
um die Wahrheit zu sagen	to tell the truth
Witze / Geschichten erzählen	tell jokes / stories

→ MERKE!

- ***tell*** hat ein Personenobjekt oder ein abstraktes Objekt — *Anne told me (that) she was too tired to tell stories / jokes. Are you telling the truth?*
- ***say*** hat *kein* direktes Personenobjekt; Personen werden mit to angeschlossen — *Anne said (that) she was tired. What did he say to you?*

The specialist's CORNER

Sag es mir.	Tell me. (*kein* it)
sagen, was man denkt	speak one's mind
ein Gebet sprechen	say a prayer
das kann man wohl sagen	you can say that again

mean* = sagen im Sinne von *bedeuten

Das sagt mir nichts.	It doesn't mean a thing to me.
Sagt dir das etwas?	Does that mean anything to you?

JOKE YOUR WAY round trouble spots

Is it *say* or *tell*?

1. "You look worried. What did the doctor ____________?"
   "He ____________ me to take these pills for the rest of my life."
   "So, what's the problem?"
   "He only gave me half a dozen."
2. The drunk approached the policeman. "Officer, can you ____________ me where I am?"

"You are on the corner of Main Street and Chester Avenue."
"Forget the details. What town is it?"

3. Do you ______________ a prayer before you eat?
No, we don't have to. My mother is a good cook.

92 schön – *beautiful, fair, handsome* oder *fine*?

TEST YOURSELF : Which word fits best?

1. The two of them make a ________________ couple.
2. You don't have to be young to be ________________.
3. He has a very ________________ wife.
4. That's a very ________________ piece of furniture.

TROUBLESHOOT your English

***beautiful* für weibliche Schönheiten und vollendet schöne Dinge**	
eine schöne Frau, Aussicht	a beautiful woman / view
ein schönes Gedicht	a beautiful poem
Das haben Sie schön gesagt!	What a beautiful thing to say!
***handsome* für schöne Männer und noble Dinge**	
schöne / gut aussehende Männer	handsome / good-looking men
ein schönes / anständiges Gehalt	a handsome salary
ein schönes Möbelstück	a handsome piece of furniture
ein schönes Geschenk / Pferd	a handsome present / horse
***pretty* = hübsch für Mädchen, Tiere und Sachen**	
ein hübsches Mädchen	a pretty girl

→ MERKE!

- ***pretty*** wird oft ironisch gebraucht:
  a pretty mess! — eine schöne Geschichte!
  it costs a pretty penny — es kostet eine schöne Stange Geld

The specialist's CORNER

das schöne Geschlecht	the fair sex
schönes Wetter	fair / fine weather
die schönen Künste	the fine arts
Schönes Wochenende!	Have a nice weekend!

JOKE YOUR WAY round trouble spots

What's the best word for *schön*?

1. "I can't believe that John is in hospital. Only yesterday I saw him with a ____________ young blonde girl in a French restaurant." "So did his wife!"
2. A woman said to the mother of a girl: "Oh, what a ____________ little girl. Is your husband ____________?"
3. The young man asked the ____________ girl to marry him. He mentioned that his father was 98 and very rich. She became his stepmother[1].
4. Tom offered a thousand-dollar reward[2] for the return of his wife's cat. Fred remarked that this was a very ____________ reward for a cat. "No problem, I drowned[3] it," said Tom.

93 schon und noch nicht – *already* oder *yet*?

TEST YOURSELF : What is it in English?

1. Hast du *schon* gefrühstückt? ________________
2. Ja, ich habe *schon* gefrühstückt. ________________
3. Geh *noch nicht*. ________________

1 Stiefmutter 2 Belohnung 3 ertränken

TROUBLESHOOT your English

***already* = schon in bejahten Aussagen**	
Ich habe schon gegessen.	I've already eaten.
Ich bin schon / bereits spät dran.	I'm already late.

- *Already* und *yet* (auf die Gegenwart bezogen) werden häufig mit *Present Perfect* gebraucht. Dabei wird *'schon'* meist nicht übersetzt. Es ist im *Present Perfect* bereits enthalten.

  Hast du schon gehört? — Have you heard?

***yet* = schon in Fragen; *not yet* = noch nicht**	
Hast du schon gegessen?	Have you eaten yet?
Ich weiß noch nicht.	I don't know yet.
Ich habe ihn noch nicht gesehen.	I haven't seen him yet.

- *already* statt *yet* drückt in verneinten und fragenden Sätzen Überraschung aus:

  Ist es schon 10 Uhr? — Is it 10 o'clock already?
  Willst du schon gehen? — You're not leaving already, are you?

The specialist's CORNER

schon bald / früher oder später	before long
schon am nächsten Tag	the very next day
schon von Anfang an	right from the start

JOKE YOUR WAY round trouble spots

What is it in English?

1. Then there was the Irishman who refused to buy a pocket calculator. He (*schon*) knew how many pockets he had.
2. Ron: Sold your house (*schon*)?
   Bob: No. After reading the agent's description, we've decided not to sell. It seems to be exactly the home we've been looking for!

3. Father: Why don't you go for a run around the block?
   Son: Why? I'm (*schon*) here.
4. An optimist thinks the glass is half full. The pessimist thinks it's half empty. The realist knows that (*schon bald*) he'll have to wash the glass.

94 Schuld – *debt, fault* oder *guilt*?

TEST YOURSELF : Which word fits best?

1. The jury has to decide on the defendant's[1] __________ or innocence[2].
2. We were poor but we have never got into __________.
3. It was his __________ that we were late.

TROUBLESHOOT your English

debt(s) = Geldschulden	
seine Schulden bezahlen	pay / settle one's debts
bis zu den Ohren in Schulden stecken	be up to one's ears in debt

→ MERKE!

jemandem etwas schulden	owe someone (some) money

guilt = Schuld im Gegensatz zu Unschuld	
Mitschuld	joint guilt
ein Schuldgefühl	a sense of guilt
Schuldkomplex	guilt complex
***fault, blame* = moralische Schuld / Verantwortung**	
Es ist nicht meine Schuld.	It's not my fault. / I'm not to blame.
die Schuld für ... auf sich nehmen	take the blame for ...

1 Angeklagte(r) 2 Unschuld

The specialist's CORNER

ein Fehler im Alarmsystem	a fault in the alarm system
Ich liebe sie trotz ihrer Fehler.	I love her for all her faults.
Schuld und Sühne	sin and atonement

JOKE YOUR WAY round trouble spots

What is it in English?

1. Sign in the window of a pawnshop[1]: "Come in! Don't be shy! Borrow your way out of (*Schulden*)!"
2. Boss: I hope you don't mind me saying this, but there's a lot of dust on the desks! It looks as if they haven't been cleaned for months. Cleaning lady: Don't (*geben Sie mir die Schuld*), sir. I have only been here for a week.
3. "Don't worry," a patient told his psychiatrist. "I'll pay every penny I (*schulde*), or my name isn't Alexander the Great!"

95 schwer – *difficult, hard* oder *heavy*?

TEST YOURSELF : Correct the two mistakes

1. In the museum visitors' book, under the heading "Reason for visit", someone had written: "*Hard* rain."
2. Just leave the most *difficult* problems for the laziest managers to solve. They will come up with the quickest solutions.
3. Work smarter – not *heavier.*

1 Pfandleiher

TROUBLESHOOT your English

- ***difficult*** = **schwierig, kompliziert** (Gegenteil: *easy* = einfach, leicht[1])

eine schwere / leichte Frage	a difficult / easy question
es ist schwer zu verstehen	it's difficult to understand

- ***hard*** = **schwer**, *beschwerlich, anstrengend*

ein schweres / leichtes Leben	a hard / easy life
schwere Zeiten	hard times
schwer arbeiten	work hard

- ***heavy*** = **schwer** an Gewicht; (Gegenteil: *light*)

ein schwerer / leichter Koffer	a heavy / light suitcase
schwer wie Blei	as heavy as lead
leicht wie eine Feder	as light as a feather

➜ MERKE:

In der Bedeutung von *schwierig* sind *hard* und *difficult* oft austauschbar; *hard* ist weniger förmlich als *difficult*.

Nowadays it is *difficult / hard* to go on a honeymoon[2] because it's *difficult / hard* to find a baby-sitter.

The specialist's CORNER

schwere Verletzungen	severe injuries
ein schwerer Schock	a severe / terrible shock
eine schwere Behinderung	a severe handicap

➜ ACHTUNG!

er ist achtzig Kilo schwer	he weighs eighty kilos
ein zwei Pfund schwerer Fisch	a two-pound fish

1 siehe auch „leicht", Seite 102 2 Flitterwochen

JOKE YOUR WAY round trouble spots

What is it?

hard • difficult • heavy

1. "Doctor, doctor! Everybody thinks I'm a liar[1]."
   "Hmmmm! I find this very ____________ to believe."
2. It's ____________ to get a man to understand something when his salary depends upon[2] his not understanding it.
3. "This letter is too ____________ . You have to put more stamps[3] on."
   "And that will make it lighter?"
4. It's very ____________ to work with my accountant[4]. Every time we're getting somewhere, the guard[5] says, "Visiting time's over."

96 (an-, aus-, zu-) sehen – *look, see* oder *watch*?

TEST YOURSELF: Which word fits best?

1. Tact is the ability to describe others as they ____________ themselves.
2. A Trabi makes your average[6] Skoda ____________ like a Ferrari.
3. The boss is the only one who _________ the clock during a coffee break.

TROUBLESHOOT your English

***see* = sehen, erkennen, (ungewollt) wahrnehmen**	
Ich kann nichts sehen.	I can't see anything.
Blinde können nicht sehen.	Blind people cannot see.

1 Lügner 2 abhängen von 3 Briefmarken 4 Buchhalter 5 Gefängniswärter 6 Durchschnitts-

watch = **zuschauen; beobachten**	
fernsehen	watch TV
Vögel beobachten	watch birds
das Pokalendspiel ansehen	watch the cup final
look = (bewusst) **nach etwas sehen; aussehen**	
Sieh nur! Sehen Sie mal!	Look!
auf die Uhr sehen	look at one's watch
Du siehst blass aus.	You look pale.

The specialist's CORNER

Mal sehen!	Let me see!
siehe oben / unten	see above / below
Ich sehe die Sache anders.	I see it differently.

JOKE YOUR WAY round trouble spots

What is it in English? Mind the verb forms.

1. If you like laws and sausages[1], you should never (*zuschauen*) either one being made. OTTO VON BISMARCK
2. "Waiter! Waiter! (*Schauen Sie*)! What is this fly doing in my soup?" "Hum ... (*aussehen*) like breaststroke[2], doesn't it?"
3. Policeman: When I (*sehen*) you coming round that bend[3] I thought: Forty-five at least.
   Woman driver: Well, I always (*aussehen*) older in this hat.
4. Dolly asked Priscilla why she had given up her boyfriend. "I (*sehen*) him at the swimming pool one day," she said, "and he (*aussehen*) so different without his wallet[4]."
5. A small boy was (*zusehen*) his Mum do the washing. "Mum, where did you work before you got this job here with us?"

1 Gesetze und Würste 2 Brustschwimmen 3 Kurve 4 Brieftasche

97 seit – *since* oder *for*?

TEST YOURSELF : Right or Wrong?

	R	W
1. I have been playing squash *since* ten years.		
2. I've known Joanna *since* she was born.		
3. A doctor to his patient: "I've been giving you medicine for yellow fever *since* four weeks and now you tell me that you're Chinese."		

TROUBLESHOOT your English

since = **seit** einem Zeitpunkt oder Ereignis	
seit wann?	since when?
seit ich ihn zum letzten Mal gesehen habe	since I last saw him
seit ich geboren bin	since I was born
***for* = seit mit Zeitraum**	
seit einem Jahr	for a year
seit langem	for a long time
seit einer Ewigkeit	for ages

→ MERKE:

Situationen, die in der Vergangenheit begonnen haben und bis zum Zeitpunkt des Sprechens andauern, werden mit dem *Present Perfect (Progressive)* ausgedrückt. Im Deutschen steht meist Präsens.

Er wohnt seit drei Jahren in Bonn. He has lived in Bonn for three years.

→ ACHTUNG! Einleitendes *since* kann auch *da / weil* bedeuten.

Since a politician never believes what he says,
he is always astonished when others do. CHARLES DE GAULLE

JOKE YOUR WAY round trouble spots

Is it *since* or *for*?

1. I haven't been so upset[1] __________ Margaret asked me what I wanted to name the baby. Margaret – that's my secretary.
2. We were married successfully __________ four years. Then my wife lost her job.
3. Patient: Aren't these pills habit-forming[2]?
   Doctor: Rubbish, I've been taking them __________ years.
4. "And how long have you believed in reincarnation?"
   "Ever __________ I was a frog."
5. "I have been in love with the same woman __________ forty years. If my wife finds out she'll kill me." HENRY YOUNGMAN

98 sicher – *safe(ly), sure(ly)* oder *certain(ly)*?

TEST YOURSELF : Which word fits best?

1. It's my firm belief that I and the Pope are infallible[3] – although[4] I'm not ________________ about him.
2. Cars made in Britain are absolutely ________________ and reliable; they have been approved to British Standards BS 9966. (But so was the Titanic.)
3. "How long has old Pedro been fishing?" – "I'm not ________________, but he's the only member of the angling club fishing with a Louis XV rod[5]."

1 schockiert 2 süchtig machen 3 unfehlbar 4 obwohl 5 Angelrute

TROUBLESHOOT your English

→ Der Gebrauch von ***sure*** / ***certain*** hängt von der Sicht des Sprechers ab.

be sure / surely = subjektiv **sicher sein**	
Ich bin sicher, er kommt.	I'm sure he will come.
Du hast seinen Brief sicher schon gelesen.	You've surely read his letter.
be certain / certainly = objektiv (ganz) **sicher/ überzeugt sein**	
Ich weiß ganz sicher, dass ich die Rechnung bezahlt habe.	I know for certain / I'm positive that I paid the bill.
Ich heirate Tom ganz sicher nicht.	I'm certainly not going to marry Tom.
be safe / safely = **unversehrt, sicher** vor Gefahren sein	
Die Leiter ist nicht sicher.	The ladder is not safe.
Ich kam sicher und unverletzt an.	I arrived safe and sound.
Das brennende Flugzeug landete sicher.	The burning plane landed safely.

The specialist's CORNER

sichergehen / sich vergewissern	make sure
ganz sicher sein	be positive / certain
Diese Brücke ist nicht sicher.	This bridge is not secure.

JOKE YOUR WAY round trouble spots

What is it in English?

1. Lawyer: Are you (*sicher*) that the defendant[1] is the man who stole your car?
   Witness[2]: Well, I was until you cross-examined me. Now I'm not (*sicher*) whether I had a car at all.
2. The American West is a place where men are men, but in San Francisco you can never be (*sicher*).

1 Angeklagte(r) 2 Zeuge

3. Psychiatrist to patient: "You have nothing to worry about. Anyone who can pay my bills is (*sicher*) not a failure."
4. Banks are closing by the hundreds today. If you want to rob one, (*sich vergewissern*) you call first to see if it's still open.
5. Old lady to pilot: Please bring us down (*sicher*).
   Pilot: Don't worry, lady, I haven't left anybody up there yet.
6. Graffiti: The only (*sichere*) fast breeder[1] is a rabbit[2].
   No to NUCLEAR POWER!

99 so – *so, such* oder *like this / that*?

TEST YOURSELF : What is it in English?

1. Ich bin nicht *so* dumm, das zu glauben.
   I'm not __________ stupid as to believe that.
2. Es ist *so* schade, dass du nicht bei uns sein kannst.
   It's __________ a pity that you can't be with us.
3. Ich habe *so* etwas noch nie gehört.
   I've never heard __________ a thing.
4. Ich wollte, wir hätten *so* ein Haus.
   I wish we had a house __________.

TROUBLESHOOT your English

so **steht vor Adjektiv oder Adverb**	
Schau nicht so böse.	Don't look so angry.
Er saß so ruhig da!	He sat there so quietly!
um so besser	so much the better

1 Schneller Brüter 2 Kaninchen

such **steht vor Adjektiv plus Substantiv**	
Es ist so ein schöner Tag!	It's such a beautiful day!
Sie ist so eine intelligente Frau.	She's such an intelligent woman.
like (this / that) **steht in Vergleichen**	
Schau! So musst du es machen.	Look! You must do it like this.
Schau mich nicht so an.	Don't look at me like that.
Niemand konnte so Gitarre spielen wie er.	No one could play the guitar like he did.

The specialist's CORNER

So ein Idiot!	What / Such an idiot!
doppelt so viele	twice as many
so ist das Leben	that's life / such is life

JOKE YOUR WAY round trouble spots

such • so • like that

1. "Why is your dog staring at me __________?" – "Probably because you're eating from his dish."
2. One charter flight was __________ crowded, the pilot went by boat!
3. Boss: How can one person make __________ many mistakes in a single day?
   Secretary: I get up early.
4. He is __________ a bore, even my legs fall asleep when he talks.

100 sollen – *be meant to, ought to, shall, should* oder *be supposed to*?

TEST YOURSELF : What is it in English?

1. What (*sollen*) we do this weekend?
2. You (*solltest nicht*) drink and drive.
3. You (*hättest hören sollen*) to the warnings.
4. (*Es sollte sein*) an apology[1] but it only made her angry.

TROUBLESHOOT your English

shall **für Bitten um Rat und Anweisungen**	
Wo soll ich mein Rad hinstellen?	Where shall I put my bike?
Was soll ich nun tun?	What shall I do now?
be to **für Frage nach und Weitergabe von Anweisungen**	
Wir sollen nicht auf dem Rasen spielen.	We aren't to play on the lawn.
Soll Tom das Auto waschen?	Is Tom to wash the car?
be supposed to **für Pflichten und Vereinbarungen**	
Ich soll ihn anrufen.	I'm supposed to ring him up.
Er hätte teilnehmen sollen.	He was supposed to take part.
ought to / should **für moralische Pflichten**	
Du solltest dich schämen.	You ought to be ashamed.
Ich hätte es wissen sollen.	I should have known.
be meant to **für Zweck und Absicht**	
Das soll ein Geschenk sein.	This is meant to be a present.
Es sollte ein Witz sein.	It was meant as a joke.
be said / believed / supposed to **für Gerüchte und Meinungen**	
Er soll reich sein.	He is said to be rich.
Er soll tot sein.	He is believed to be dead.

1 Entschuldigung

The specialist's CORNER

Was soll's?	So what / Who cares?
Du sollst nicht töten.	Thou shalt not kill.
Es hat nicht sein sollen.	It just wasn't meant to be.
Das sollst du mir büßen!	I'll make you pay for that.
Es soll nicht wieder vorkommen.	It won't happen again.

JOKE YOUR WAY round trouble spots

be meant to • ought to • be supposed to • shall • should

1. Angry employer: You ______________ have been here at nine o'clock.
   Late employee: Why, what happened?
2. Patient: ______________ I start at the beginning?
   Doctor: Please do so.
   Patient: Well, in the beginning I created Heaven and Earth.
3. Mum: Dad, you ______________ take Jimmy to the zoo today.
   Dad: Not me! If the zoo wants him, they can come and get him!
4. The Commandments don't tell you what you ______________ do: they only put ideas into your head. ELIZABETH BIBESCO
5. If man had been ______________ fly, he would have been born with wings.

101 suchen – *look for, search (for)* oder *seek*?

TEST YOURSELF : Which phrase for *suchen* fits best?

1. I spent most of the morning ______________ my passport.
2. He ______________ desperately for something to say.
3. I think it's time we ______________ legal advice.
4. Passengers are regularly ______________ before they board a plane.

TROUBLESHOOT your English

look for = **suchen** (allgemein), Ausschau halten nach	
Pilze suchen	look for mushrooms
Du wirst gesucht.	They're looking for you.
etwas Bestimmtes suchen	look for something particular
search for = (intensiv) **suchen, fahnden, forschen**	
nach Waffen suchen	search for weapons
auf der Suche nach Wahrheit	in search of truth
search = **durchsuchen**	
im Internet suchen	search the Net
ein Haus durchsuchen	search a house
ein Durchsuchungsbefehl	a search warrant
seek, sought, sought = (gehobener Stil) **ersuchen, bitten, erstreben, begehren, trachten**	
Rat suchen	seek advice
Obdach suchen	seek shelter
Abenteuer suchen	seek adventure

The specialist's CORNER

das Weite suchen	take to one's heels
Was suchen Sie hier?	What are you doing here?
Sie haben hier nichts zu suchen.	You have no business being here.

JOKE YOUR WAY round trouble spots

look for • search • search for

1. A theologian is a blind man in a dark room who is ____________ a black cat which is not there – and finds it.
2. The sales manager of a large export firm received news one morning that one of his top salesmen had died in Milan. He immediately sent a fax to the Milan office: "Return samples[1] by airmail and ____________ the body for orders[2]."
3. A secretary is a young and attractive lady who is paid to learn how to type letters while she is ____________ a husband.

1 Muster 2 Aufträge

102 Tasche – *bag, briefcase* oder *pocket*?

TEST YOURSELF : What is it in English?

1. Our boss expects us to pay for the trip out of our own (*Taschen*).
2. She opened her (*Handtasche*) and took out her comb.
3. I left my (*Aktentasche*) in the office.
4. When is your book coming out (*als Taschenbuch*)?

TROUBLESHOOT your English

pocket = **Tasche** in Kleidungsstücken	
in die eigene Tasche wirtschaften	line one's own pockets
ein Taschenwörterbuch	a pocket dictionary
Taschendieb	pickpocket
Taschenrechner	pocket calculator
bag = **Tasche** (in Zusammensetzungen), **Tüte**	
Schultasche	schoolbag
Handtasche	(hand-)bag
Einkaufstasche	shopping bag
etwas in der Tasche haben	have something in the bag

The specialist's CORNER

Aktentasche, Aktenkoffer	briefcase / attaché case
Akten-, Dokumentenmappe	folder
Brieftasche	wallet
Taschenbuch	paperback
Taschentuch	handkerchief

→ MERKE: *a map* ist keine *Mappe*, sondern eine *Landkarte*

JOKE YOUR WAY round trouble spots

Which word fits the context best?

bag • handbag • pocket • wallet

1. Just when you think you've got the promotion[1] in the ____________, some new guy will come along and marry the boss's daughter.
2. A fellow says, "In Florida they use alligators to make ____________." His friend says, "Isn't it amazing what they can get animals to do?"
3. Then there was the Irishman who refused[2] to buy a ____________ calculator. He already knew how many ____________ he had.
4. Inflation is when ____________ are getting bigger and shopping ____________ smaller.

103 Termin – *appointment, date* oder *deadline*?

TEST YOURSELF : Right or Wrong?

	R	W
1. I've got an *appointment* with Tina. I asked her out for dinner.		
2. I'd like to make an *appointment* with your doctor.		
3. Call my secretary and arrange a *date*.		
4. The *appointment* for applications[3] is 30 April.		
5. Should we set a *date* for the next meeting?		

1 Beförderung 2 sich weigern 3 Bewerbungen

TROUBLESHOOT your English

***appointment* = Termin, Verabredung mit jemandem**	
Termine einhalten müssen	have to keep appointments
ein Termin beim Arzt	an appointment with the doctor
einen Termin stornieren	cancel an appointment
***date* = Termin, Datum, an dem etwas geschehen soll**	
einen Termin festlegen	set a date for a meeting
ein Treffen verabreden	arrange a date
***date* = (romantische) Verabredung, Rendezvous**	
sich mit Mädchen verabreden	to date girls
Mit wem bist du verabredet?	Who is your date?
***deadline* = letzter Termin, Frist**	
den Termin / die Frist einhalten	meet the deadline
jemanden eine Frist setzen	set someone a deadline

JOKE YOUR WAY round trouble spots

1. I had (*einen Termin*) with my doctor this morning. He gave me six months to live, but when I couldn't pay the bill[1] he gave me another six months. WALTER MATTHAU
2. Bisexuality immediately doubles your chances of a (*Verabredung*) on Saturday night. WOODY ALLEN
3. A man called his doctor for (*einen Termin*). "I'm sorry," said the man, "but I could be dead by then!" – "No problem. If your wife lets us know, we'll cancel (*den Termin*)."

1 Rechnung

104 tragen – *bear, carry* oder *wear*?

TEST YOURSELF : Right or Wrong?

	R	W
1. Police in many countries *wear* guns.		
2. He can't *bear* to be laughed at.		
3. Do I have to *wear* a tie?		
4. She *carries* the responsibility for most of the changes.		

TROUBLESHOOT your English

***carry* = mit sich tragen von Gegenständen**	
einen Koffer tragen	carry a suitcase
Waffen tragen	carry guns
Ich trage nie viel Geld mit mir herum.	I never carry much money on me.
***wear* = tragen von Kleidern, Schmuck, Haar etc.**	
eine Brille tragen	wear glasses / spectacles
eine Krawatte tragen	wear a tie
einen Bart tragen	wear a beard
Sie trägt ihr Haar lang.	She wears her hair long.
bear (bore, born) = (er)tragen im übertragenen Sinn	
Früchte tragen	bear fruit
die Verantwortung tragen	bear the responsibility
Kosten tragen	bear the costs
Geduld haben mit	bear with someone / something

JOKE YOUR WAY round trouble spots

What is the English for *tragen*? Mind the form of the verbs.

1. Our modern world is so full of problems that if Moses came down from Mount Sinai again, the two tablets[1] he'd be ________________ would be aspirins.
2. A manager is someone who ________________ more responsibility than power.
3. Some Friesians still think that a transistor is a priest who likes ________________ women's clothes.
4. I put the wrong size of batteries in the beeper that I ______________ on my belt. The first call I got blew my shoes off.

1 Tafel, Tablette

105 übersehen – *look over, overlook* oder *oversee*?

TEST YOURSELF : Match the numbers and the letters

A. Blick haben auf	B. durchsehen	C. ignorieren
D. besichtigen	E. überwachen	F. übersehen

1. I seem to have *overlooked* one important fact. ____
2. We *looked over* the house again before we decided to rent it. ____
3. Our hotel *overlooked* the lake. ____
4. I'm not prepared to *overlook* his behaviour. ____
5. The government agency *oversees* the airport. ____
6. He's *looking over* the photos he'd taken the day before. ____

TROUBLESHOOT your English

● ***overlook***

1. **übersehen, ignorieren**:
   Fehler übersehen: overlook mistakes
2. **überblicken**:
   ein Zimmer mit Blick auf den See: a room overlooking the lake

● ***oversee***: **überwachen, überprüfen, kontrollieren**

ein Projekt überwachen: oversee a project

● ***look over***: **prüfend anschauen, durchsehen, besichtigen**

mögliche Bauplätze besichtigen: look over possible building sites

The specialist's CORNER

etwas absichtlich übersehen	turn a blind eye to something
versehentlich übersehen	escape someone's notice

JOKE YOUR WAY round trouble spots

Which verb fits best?

oversee • overlook • look over

1. The garage mechanic ________________ Ernie's car and said: "If I were you I'd keep the oil and change the car."
2. Seaside landlady: The only rooms we have at the moment ________________ the sea. They're £5 a night extra.
   Holidaymaker: How much if I promise not to look?
3. One payday, an employee received an unusually large cheque[1], and decided not to say anything about it. The following week, her cheque was for less than the normal sum, and she confronted her boss. "How come," the boss asked, "you didn't say anything when you were overpaid?" Unruffled[2], the employee replied, "Well, I can ________________ one mistake, but not two in a row[3]!"

106 Übung / üben – *exercise* oder *practice*?

TEST YOURSELF : What is it in English?

1. She's (*üben*) for her piano exam.
2. Have you done your piano (*Übungen*) yet?
3. It takes a lot of (*Übung*) to play the violin well.
4. Roll over and repeat the (*Übung*) on the other leg.

1 Gehaltsabrechnung 2 gelassen 3 hintereinander

TROUBLESHOOT your English

practice **= regelmäßige Übung**, um sich zu perfektionieren	
Übung macht den Meister.	Practice makes perfect.
Du musst jeden Tag üben.	You need to practise every day.
in / außer Übung sein	be in / be out of practice
exercise **= Einzelübung** oder körperliche Betätigung	
ein Übungsbuch	an exercise book
Fitnessübungen	keep-fit exercises
Du solltest dich mehr bewegen.	You should take more exercise.
Pferde müssen regelmäßig bewegt werden.	Horses need to be exercised regularly.

The specialist's CORNER

Medizin praktizieren	practise medicine
eine Arztpraxis	a doctor's practice
neue Ideen in die Praxis umsetzen	put new ideas into practice
in Übung bleiben	keep one's hand in

JOKE YOUR WAY round trouble spots

Is it *exercise* or *practice*?

1. It takes a lot of ____________ for a girl to kiss like a beginner.
2. The best way to stay young is eat well, ____________ and lie about your age.
3. A specialist is a doctor with a smaller ____________ but a bigger yacht.
4. ____________ makes perfect, but that's no consolation[1] if you are the dentist's first patient.

1 Trost

107 unter – *among, below, beneath* oder *under*?

TEST YOURSELF : Right or Wrong?

	R	W
1. Have you looked *below* the bed?		
2. He was *among* the last to leave.		
3. Someone was having a party in the flat *under*.		
4. He dived *below* the surface of the water.		
5. They thought she had married *under* her.		

TROUBLESHOOT your English

under = **unter** Dingen, Einflüssen stehen	
unter dem Einfluss von Alkohol	under the influence of alcohol
unter achtzehn (Jahren)	under eighteen
unter Aufsicht	under supervision

- ***under*** kann (im Gegensatz zu *beneath, below*) für die Bewegungsrichtung verwendet werden:

  Wir schwammen unter der Brücke durch. We swam under the bridge.

- ***beneath*** ist literarischer als ***under***

  unter meiner Würde beneath my dignity

- ***beneath*** und ***below*** können allein stehen, ***under*** nicht

below = **unter** einem Messwert; unterhalb	
unter dem Durchschnitt	below average
10 Grad unter null	10 degrees below zero
unter der Oberfläche	below the surface

among = unter anderem, zwischen, inmitten	
unter anderem	among other things
unter Freunden sein	be among friends
ein Haus zwischen den Bäumen	a house among the trees

The specialist's CORNER

was versteht man unter...?	what is meant by ...?
unter der Woche	during the week
einer unter hundert	one in a hundred
einer unter vielen	one of many

JOKE YOUR WAY round trouble spots

Fill in the missing words for German *unter*.

1. ________ the books with unhappy endings are cheque books.
2. He entered the vet's[1] clinic with a cat ________ his arm. "It's been as sick as a dog," he said.
3. ________ capitalism man exploits[2] man; ________ socialism the reverse[3] is true.
4. Sign in a lavatory: "Please use the toilet brush." Someone had written ________: "I tried, but now I've gone back to using paper."

1 Tierarztpraxis 2 ausbeuten 3 Gegenteil

108 verdienen – *earn* oder *deserve*?

TEST YOURSELF : Spot the mistakes

1. You are *deserving* a rest after all that hard work.
2. All my children are *earning* now.
3. They didn't *earn* to win.
4. She *deserved* a living as a part-time secretary.

TROUBLESHOOT your English

***earn* = Geld verdienen**	
gut verdienen	earn a good / decent salary
ein Vermögen verdienen	make / earn a fortune
***deserve* = Lob, Tadel, Strafe verdienen**	
Womit habe ich das verdient?	What have I done to deserve that?
eine Pause verdient haben	deserve a break

→ MERKE: *deserve* steht in der Regel nicht in der Verlaufsform.

The specialist's CORNER

- ***merit***: Lob, Tadel verdienen, einer Sache Wert sein

  merit ist seltener als *deserve*:

  Der Fall verdient weitere Betrachtung.
  The case merits further consideration.

- ***earn***: *ernten, verdienen* als Ergebnis einer guten Tat oder Eigenschaft

  Er verdiente sich den Respekt seiner Studenten.
  He earned the respect of his students.

JOKE YOUR WAY round trouble spots

What is it in English?

1. Democracy is a system that ensures[1] that we shall be governed no better than we (*verdienen*). G. B. SHAW
2. The income tax authorities[2] have made up a new tax form with only two lines:
   1. How much do you (*verdienen*)? 2. Send it.
3. Lady: Young man, I am going to give you a dollar not because you (*verdienen*) it, but because it pleases me to do so.
   Beggar[3]: Thanks, but why not make it 10 dollars so you can really enjoy yourself?

109 Versuch / versuchen – *attempt, experiment* oder *try*?

TEST YOURSELF : What is it in English?

1. Many people do not like the idea of (*Versuche*) on animals.
2. It's his fourth (*Versuch*) at breaking the world record.
3. I doubt they'll be able to help but it's worth a (*Versuch*).

TROUBLESHOOT your English

try = **Versuch, versuchen** (allgemein)	
Du hast es nicht einmal versucht.	You haven't even tried.
Es käme auf einen Versuch an.	We could give it a try.
Es ist einen Versuch wert.	It's worth a try.
attempt = **Versuch, versuchen** (mit Risiko und Mühe)	
einen Fluchtversuch unternehmen	attempt an escape
beim ersten Versuch Erfolg haben	succeed at the first attempt
Versuche nicht, es selber zu reparieren.	Do not attempt to repair this yourself.

1 garantieren 2 Finanzamt 3 Bettler

***experiment* = Versuch in Wissenschaft und Wirtschaft**	
Laborversuche	laboratory experiments
ein Experiment machen mit	to do / perform / carry out / conduct an experiment on
mit Tieren experimentieren	experiment on animals

The specialist's CORNER

- *einen Versuch machen*: make an attempt, *aber*: have a try

→ In der Struktur *try and do something* kann *try* nur in der Grundform oder der Befehlsform stehen.

Try and finish quickly. *Aber*: He *tried to* finish quickly.

- *es* versuchen: das *es* fällt im Englischen weg.

Du hast es nicht versucht. Lass mich es versuchen.
You haven't tried. Let me try.

JOKE YOUR WAY round trouble spots

attempt • experiment • try

1. Having had an argument[1] with your boss, any __________ to improve relations[2] makes it worse.
2. A woman lion tamer had the cats under such control that they took a lump of sugar from her lips on command. The ringmaster came over and asked Tom, "Would you like to have a __________?" – "Certainly," said Tom. "But first get those crazy lions out of there."
3. In an __________ to boost sales[3], British Airways announced that for two weeks, any business executive could take his wife along with him for only twenty per cent of the normal fare. In order to judge the success of this __________ they wrote to all the wives concerned, asking them if they had enjoyed their flights. Eighty-five percent of the wives wrote back asking, "What flight?"

1 Streit 2 Beziehungen verbessern 3 Verkauf ankurbeln

110 wählen – *choose, elect, select* oder *vote*?

TEST YOURSELF : Right or Wrong?

	R	W
1. He hasn't been *elected* for the team.		
2. How did you *choose* at the last election?		
3. Over 60% of members *elected* in favour of the candidate.		
4. There are plenty of restaurants to *choose* from.		

TROUBLESHOOT your English

***choose, chose, chosen* = wählen, aussuchen**	
seine Worte sorgfältig wählen	choose one's words carefully
Er wählte eine rote Krawatte.	He chose a red tie.
Du hast klug gewählt.	You've made a wise choice.
***elect someone* = jemanden (in ein Amt) wählen**	
einen Führer wählen	elect a leader
für fünf Jahre gewählt werden	be elected for a period of five years
die Präsidentschaftswahlen	the presidential elections
***select* = sorgfältig auswählen**	
die Teilnehmer auswählen	select the members for a team
ein Auswahlprozess	a selection process
***vote for* = jemanden wählen, für ihn stimmen**	
ins Parlament gewählt werden	be voted into parliament
für oder gegen jemanden stimmen	vote for or against someone
Stimmen wir ab!	Let's have a vote!

The specialist's CORNER

wählen gehen	go to the polls
eine (Telefon-)Nummer wählen	dial a number

JOKE YOUR WAY round trouble spots

What is it in English?

1. In any organisation it is more important to (*wählen*) your enemies than it is to (*wählen*) your friends.
2. If (*wählen*) changed anything, they'd make it illegal.
3. A jury consists of twelve persons (*gewählt*) to decide who has the better lawyer. ROBERT FROST
4. Why did God give all the oil to the Arabs and all the kangaroos to the Australians? – Well, the Australians had first (*Wahl*).

111 während – *during* oder *while*?

TEST YOURSELF : What is it in English?

1. I only saw her once (*während*) my stay in Rome.
2. We repair your car (*während*) you wait.
3. (*Während*) the summer season, all the hotels are full.
4. You can go swimming (*während*) I'm having lunch.

TROUBLESHOOT your English

***during* = während steht vor Substantiven**	
während der Sitzung	during the meeting
während seines Besuchs	during his visit
während der Hauptsaison	during the peak season

***while* = während steht vor Verben und Nebensätzen**	
während er sprach	while he was speaking
Jemand hat angerufen, während du weg warst.	Someone called while you were out.

→ ACHTUNG!

- *While* steht auch, wenn das Verb durch Satzverkürzung wegfällt.

While in prison he shared a cell with Ron. (*While* he *was* in prison ...)
While in Canada she married Bert. (*While* she was staying ...)

The specialist's CORNER

***Während* = while kann im Englischen und im Deutschen auch einen Gegensatz oder Unterschied ausdrücken.**

The west of Germany grows richer, *while* the east grows poorer.
Der Westen Deutschlands wird reicher, während der Osten ärmer wird.

JOKE YOUR WAY round trouble spots

Is it *during* or *while*?

1. ___________ the dance the blonde says to her partner, "I'm dancing a tango, and you?"
2. No woman has ever shot her husband ___________ he was doing the dishes[1].
3. Honeymoon is the period ___________ which the bride trusts the bridegroom's word of honour.
4. There were four wise men. ___________ following the star on the way to the manger[2], one of them said he knew a short cut[3].
5. Barking dogs do not bite – ___________ barking[4].

1 Geschirr spülen 2 Krippe 3 Abkürzung 4 bellen

112 was für ein ... – *what* ... oder *what a* ...?

TEST YOURSELF : Correct these horrible mistakes

1. *Was für ein Bier ziehen Sie vor?*	What for a beer do you prefer?
2. *Was für ein Wetter!*	What a weather!
3. *Was für ein Tier ist das?*	What an animal is that?
4. *Für was interessieren Sie sich?*	In what are you interested?

TROUBLESHOOT your English

1. Frage nach Eigenschaften: ***what*** ohne Artikel	
Was für Bücher?	What (what sort / kind of) books?
Was für Leute?	What (what sort / kind of) people?
Was für eine Farbe hat Ihr Auto?	What colour is your car?
Was für ein Tier ist das?	What animal is that?
2. *What* vor Verben	
Für was interessierst du dich?	What are you interested in?
Für was brauchst du es?	What do you need it for?

→ **MERKE:** Präpositionen werden in der *What-Frage* nachgestellt.

3. ***What*** bei emotionalen Ausrufen	
Was für ein Genie!	What a genius!
Was für ein nettes Mädchen!	What a nice girl!
Was für schöne Äpfel!	What fine apples!
Was für ein Gedächtnis!	What a memory!

- Der unbestimmte Artikel *a* steht vor zählbaren Substantiven in der Einzahl: *Was für ein (tolles) Mädchen*! What *a* girl!

  Der Artikel fällt weg vor zählbaren Substantiven in der Mehrzahl.

Was für ein Wetter!	What weather!
Was für ein Unsinn!	What nonsense!
Was für ein Spaß!	What fun!

- Der unbestimmte Artikel fehlt vor nicht zählbaren Substantiven.

  Leider gibt es einige Ausnahmen:

  Was für ein Jammer! — What *a* pity!
  Was für eine Schande! — What *a* shame!

→ **VORSICHT!**

- Frage: What girl? — Was für ein / Welches Mädchen?
  Ausruf: What *a* girl! — Was für ein (tolles) Mädchen!

JOKE YOUR WAY round trouble spots

Is it *what* ... or *what a* ...?

1. ________ salesman! He sold the Venus de Milo a spray deodorant.
2. Customer: May I have a pair of alligator shoes?
   Salesman: Certainly. ________ size is your alligator?
3. Tina: I used to be young once.
   Tony: ________ memory!
4. Anne: I've just come back from the beauty salon.
   Tina: ________ pity it was closed!
5. A man walked into a police station and said: "I've come about the job that's advertised outside." – "________ job?" asked the policeman. – "The one on the poster outside that says: MAN WANTED FOR BURGLARY[1]."

1 Einbruchdiebstahl

113 wenig – *little, a little* oder *few*?

TEST YOURSELF : What is it in English?

1. Why are there so (*wenige*) women in Parliament?
2. The politician said (*wenig*) or nothing.
3. (*Wenige*) of the visitors left early.
4. There is (*wenig*) hope of finding survivors[1].

TROUBLESHOOT your English

little (less, least) vor nicht zählbaren Substantiven im Singular	
Ich habe nur wenig Geld übrig.	I have little money left.
Ich habe ein wenig Geld übrig.	I have a little money left.
der Weg des geringsten Widerstands	the path of least resistance
few (fewer, fewest) **vor zählbaren Substantiven im Plural**	
in wenigen Tagen	in a few days' time
mit wenigen Worten	in a few words
Wenige Menschen wohnen dort.	Few people live there.

- ***a few/ a little*** : *ein paar / etwas* haben gewöhnlich positive Bedeutung
  I've got *a few* questions for you. We have *a little* money left.
- ***few / little*** : *wenige / wenig* haben gewöhnlich negative Bedeutung.
  Few visitors came to the exhibition. We have *little* money left.

The specialist's CORNER

ein wenig gelesener Autor	a little read author
Das ist die geringste meiner Sorgen.	That's the least of my worries.
ein wenig übertrieben	slightly exaggerated

1 Überlebende

JOKE YOUR WAY round trouble spots

little • a little • less • few • a few

1. Call a meeting at 4.30 on Fridays and you'll get ________ opposition.
2. The battle seemed lost, so the Italian general gave his last orders. "Listen boys! When the enemy is only ________ hundred metres away you may start retreating[1]. Being ________ lame, I'll leave now."
3. Most of us know how to say nothing – ________ of us know when.
4. A man's credit card was stolen but he decided not to report it because the thief was spending ________ than his wife did.
5. You should be ________ suspicious[2] of your wife if she asks for her weekly household money in traveller's checks.

114 wenn – *if* oder *when*?

TEST YOURSELF : Right or Wrong?

	R	W
1. Don't tell lies *if* you can use statistics.		
2. *If* there's no alternative, there's no problem.		
3. Tact is the art of saying nothing *when* there is nothing to say.		
4. *If* you will look like your passport photo you really need the holiday.		
5. I will tell him *when* I will meet him tomorrow.		

1 sich zurückziehen 2 argwöhnisch

TROUBLESHOOT your English

if = wenn, falls für Bedingungen und Einzelfälle	
Wenn du ihn siehst, sag es ihm.	If you see him, tell him.
Wenn nötig, komme ich sofort.	If necessary I'll come at once.
Wenn ich das nur gewusst hätte!	If only I had known!
***when* = sobald / immer wenn (zeitlich) für Regelfälle**	
Ruf mich, wenn du fertig bist.	Call me when you've finished.
Er grüßt mich nie, wenn er mich sieht.	He never greets me when he sees me.
Sag halt!	Say when!

→ ACHTUNG!

- Im Nebensatz mit ***if*** (Bedingungssatz) steht kein Futur.
- Im Nebensatz mit ***when*** (Temporalsatz) steht ebenfalls kein Futur.
- In der Frage mit ***when*** (Wann ...?) kann jedoch Futur stehen.
  When *will* I see you again?

JOKE YOUR WAY round trouble spots

Is it *if* or *when*?

1. Why does a Lada have heated rear windscreens?
   To keep your hands warm ________ you push it.
2. My wife says she'll leave me ________ I don't throw out my computer. I'll miss her.
3. Education is ________ you read the fine print[1]. Experience is what you get ________ you don't.
4. ________ you want to make a man very angry, tell him you are going to pray[2] for him. EDGAR W. HOWE

1 das Kleingedruckte 2 beten

115 werden – *become, go, get, grow* oder *turn*?

TEST YOURSELF : Which word fits best?

Mind the form of the verb.

1. Wait till the lights ________________ green.
2. The meat ________________ off. Throw it away.
3. Divorce ________________ more and more common.
4. I forgot the keys. I think I ________________ old.

TROUBLESHOOT your English

- ***become, go, get, grow*** und ***turn*** plus Adjektiv beschreiben eine Zustandsänderung
- ***get*** ist umgangssprachlicher als das förmliche *become: get angry*
- ***go*** und ***turn*** bezeichnen drastische, plötzliche Veränderungen
- ***go*** wird meist für negative Veränderungen gebraucht: *go mad / off*, ***turn*** für Wetter- und Farbwechsel: *turn red*
- ***grow*** steht für eine langsame Veränderung: *grow old / grey / rich*

become **mit seinen häufigsten Adjektiven**	
become involved	*einbezogen werden*
become clear	*klar, deutlich werden*
become / fall ill	*krank werden*
become **steht auch vor Substantiven**	
become a teacher	*Lehrer werden*
become Prime Minister	*Premierminister werden*
get **mit seinen häufigsten Adjektiven**	
get better / worse	*besser / schlechter werden*
get pregnant	*schwanger werden*
get used to	*sich gewöhnen an*

go mit seinen häufigsten Adjektiven	
go crazy	*wahnsinnig werden*
go bald	*kahl werden*
go blind	*blind werden*
go off	*schlecht werden, verderben*
***turn* mit seinen häufigsten Adjektiven**	
turn blue	*blau werden / anlaufen*
turn red	*rot werden*
the milk has turned sour	*die Milch ist sauer geworden*

JOKE YOUR WAY round trouble spots

become • go • get • turn

1. Doctor, I think I am __________ mad. Every time I ask someone the time I get a different answer.
2. "What a lazy worker you are! Is there anything you can do quickly?" – "Let me see. Yes, there is something. I __________ tired quickly."
3. When I was a boy I was told that anybody could __________ President. I'm beginning to believe it.
4. Is he old? Even his toupee has __________ grey.

116 wie – *how* oder *what ... like*?

TEST YOURSELF : Complete the questions

1.	________ *Papagei* in English?	It's *parrot*.
2.	________ spell *parrot*.	It's spelled with double *r*.
3.	________ Tom?	He is fine.
4.	________ your new neighbour ________?	I hardly know him.

TROUBLESHOOT your English

***how?* Frage nach Befinden und subjektiven Eindrücken**	
Wie geht es Ihnen?	How are you?
Wie war euer Ausflug?	How was your trip?
Du warst in Rom? Wie war's?	You were in Rome? How was it?
***how?* Frage nach der Art und Weise oder dem Maß, Grad**	
Wie weit / groß ist es?	How far / big is it?
Wie alt sind Sie?	How old are you?
Wie macht man das?	How is it done?
***what (... like)*? Bitte um (objektive) Auskunft**	
Wie ist der neuer Chef?	What is the new boss like?
Ich war nie in Madrid. Wie ist die Stadt?	I've never been to Madrid. What is the town like?
Wie spät ist es?	What time is it?
Wie heißt das auf Englisch?	What is it in English?

→ ACHTUNG! Nicht verwechseln:

- How is Tom? — *Wie geht es Tom?*
  What is Tom like? — *Wie ist Tom (so)?*
- Nach den *Verben der sinnlichen Wahrnehmung* (*see, hear* etc.) wird das *wie* nicht übersetzt:
  Ich sah, wie er das Geld nahm. — I saw him taking the money.

The specialist's CORNER

Wie wäre es mit einem Spaziergang?	How about going for a walk?
Wie schön!	How beautiful!
Er sieht nicht wie 50 aus.	He doesn't look fifty.
Ich bin so alt wie Tom.	I'm as old as Tom.

JOKE YOUR WAY round trouble spots

Translate the German in brackets.

1. It's no fun going to the airline desk to complain[1] about lost luggage only to see the clerk (*wie er anprobiert*[2]) my clothes.
2. A true gentleman is someone who knows (*wie man spielt*) the trumpet but doesn't.
3. "(*Wie ist*) your new girlfriend?" – "She's really smart. She has brains enough for two." – "Sounds like the right girl for you."
4. "What will your picture be, Angela?" asked the teacher. "I'm drawing God," she said. "That's a difficult subject," said the teacher. "Nobody knows (*wie er aussieht*)." – "They will when I'm finished," said the girl.

1 sich beschweren 2 try on

117 zuerst – *first* oder *at first*?

TEST YOURSELF : Put in *at* where necessary

1. He's so shy. ____________ *first* he wouldn't even talk about it.
2. "Do you want a drink?" – "Later, I'll finish my work __________ *first.*"
3. Who comes ____________?
4. When did you ____________ *first* meet him?
5. I didn't like the job much ____________ *first.*

TROUBLESHOOT your English

***first* = zuerst, zunächst, an erster Stelle**	
Er kam zuerst.	He was the first to arrive.
Wer zuerst kommt, mahlt zuerst.	First come, first served.
Ich habe ihn zuerst in China getroffen.	I first met him in China.
Zuallererst muss ich entscheiden, was ich anziehe.	First of all I have to decide what to wear.

- ***First*** betont die Reihenfolge: *First, ... second, ... then ...*

***at first* = zuerst, anfangs** (aber dann ...)	
Zuerst konnte ich meinen Chef nicht leiden.	At first I didn't like my boss.
Zuerst wusste ich nicht, was ich tun sollte.	At first I didn't know what to do.
Zuerst fand ich es sehr schwer.	I found it very difficult at first.

- ***At first*** betont einen Gegensatz: zuerst ... *aber* dann ...
  At first I thought he was shy, *but then* I discovered he was just not interested in other people.

JOKE YOUR WAY round trouble spots

What is it in English?

1. If (*zuerst*) you don't succeed[1], try, try again. Then give up. No use being a damned fool about it. W. C. FIELDS
2. He used to get up out of bed every morning with a headache. And his wife kept telling him, "Honey, it's feet (*zuerst*)."
3. Bank manager to young house-hunting couple: "(*Zuerst*) you tell me what you can afford[2]. Then we'll have a good laugh about it and go on from there."

1 Erfolg haben 2 sich leisten können

1 Abteil(ung)

TEST YOURSELF : Right or Wrong?

	R	W
1. This is a first-class ~~section~~ *compartment.* You've only got a second-class ticket.		✔
2. Don't ask me about our finances: that's my wife's *department.*	✔	
3. Her husband is head of the finance ~~compartment~~ *section* in the health department.		✔

JOKE YOUR WAY round trouble spots

1. "I'm sorry, Smith," said the director of a *department store* to his assistant, "but being able to skate around all nine of the *departments* completely blindfolded does not qualify you for senior management!"
2. Two men are sitting opposite each other in a train *compartment.*

2 Aktion

TEST YOURSELF : What is *action* in German?

1. You must judge people by their *actions.*	Taten
2. Her son was killed *in action* in Iraq.	im Kampf
3. The time has come *for action.*	die Zeit zu handeln

JOKE YOUR WAY round trouble spots

1. the presidential *campaign*: Wahlkampf um das Amt des Präsidenten in den USA
2. a man of *action*: ein Mann der Tat

3 aktuell

TEST YOURSELF : What is *actually* in German?

1. the *actual* state of affairs	der tatsächliche Stand der Dinge
2. the *actual* owner	der wirkliche Eigentümer
3. the *actual* film	der eigentliche Film / Hauptfilm

JOKE YOUR WAY round trouble spots

1. *Actually* there were four wise men.
2. ... unless you are *actually* drowning.
3. As soon as a program is running properly, it is no longer *up to date.*

4 alle(s)

TEST YOURSELF : Spot the mistakes and correct them

1. He rings me up ~~all~~ *every* two days.
2. He gives her *everything / all* ~~what~~ she wants.
3. We'll help *all those who* are ready to help themselves.

JOKE YOUR WAY round trouble spots

1. Tact is thinking *everything* you say without saying *everything* you think.
2. Some people will believe *anything* if you whisper it to them.
3. Self-control is when you go into a supermarket to buy a pint of milk – and *all* you buy is a pint of milk.
4. *All sorts of* computer errors are turning up now.
5. He only had to buy her a birthday present once *every four years.*

5 allein

TEST YOURSELF : Which phrase fits best?

1. Of all the applicants they *alone* had the right qualifications.
2. His secretary was on strike so he answered the letters *himself.*
3. They need help. They can't solve this problem *on their own / by themselves.*
4. Suddenly the doors seemed to open all *by themselves.*

JOKE YOUR WAY round trouble spots

1. Client: No. I prefer to be *alone.*
2. Then I found out that every time I put popcorn in my pancakes they turn over *by themselves.*
3. A: I began business *on my own.*
4. I could have done the job *myself* in twenty minutes ...

6 also

TEST YOURSELF : What is *also* in English?

1. *Also* blieb er zu Hause.	*So* he stayed at home.
2. Lassen wir's *also.*	Let's leave it *then.*
3. *Also,* wenn du mich fragst ...	*Well / Now,* if you ask me ...

4. Ich denke, *also* bin ich. — I think, *therefore* I am.
5. Sie spielt nicht nur gut, sie komponiert *auch*. — She not only plays well, but *also* writes music.

JOKE YOUR WAY round trouble spots

1. *So* you're Tom's boss.
2. Security officer: Look, there is poisonous gas in this bottle. *Now*, what steps would you take, if I dropped this bottle?
3. Our clothes not only make girls slim, they *also* make men look round.

7 ein anderer

TEST YOURSELF : Right or Wrong?

	R	W
1. She's ~~other than~~ *not like* her sister.		✔
2. He left the ~~other~~ *next / following* day.		✔
3. That's a completely *different* matter.	✔	

JOKE YOUR WAY round trouble spots

1. Love is the illusion that one man is *different from* the rest.
2. "Do you know a guy with one leg called Moloney?"
   "No. What's the name of his *other* leg?"
3. "I think I am going mad, doctor. Every time I ask someone the time I get a *different* answer."
4. "You can't resign," said the circus manager to the human cannonball. "Where would I get *another* man of your calibre?"
5. I have the feeling that my house isn't too solid. The *other day* I saw termites wearing helmets.

8 Arbeit(en)

TEST YOURSELF : What is it in English?

1. Tom, have you *done* your *homework* yet?
2. I have bought my wife the complete *works* of Tolstoy.
3. There has been an accident at the *waterworks*.

JOKE YOUR WAY round trouble spots

1. "I hate *housework,*" said the newly-wed bride.
2. I haven't done my *homework*.
3. Tim: I've heard you applied for that *job* at the film studio ...
   And did you get the *job*?

9 Art

TEST YOURSELF : What is it in English?

1. The walls were hung with all *sorts / kinds* of works of *art*.
2. She doesn't mean to be rude – it's just her *way*.
3. She's not the *kind / sort* of person to lie.

JOKE YOUR WAY round trouble spots

1. Tact: the *art* of saying nothing when there is nothing to say.
2. There are two *kinds* of statistics, the *kind* you look up and the *kind* you make up.
3. The best *way* to remember your wife's birthday is to forget it once.
4. He had the *sort* of face that makes you realise God does have a sense of humour.

10 auch

TEST YOURSELF : Right or Wrong?

	R	W
1. Adults read Harry Potter and *so* do children ~~also do~~.		✔
2. I like tennis, and I also like squash.	✔	
3. He can't hear and he can ~~either~~ hardly speak *either*.		✔

JOKE YOUR WAY round trouble spots

1. I know we're going to be happy. You adore me and *so* do I.
2. "I know, but *neither* can my neighbour if I have them!"
3. Lucy: And you ride horseback *as well / too*, don't you?

11 aufstehen

TEST YOURSELF : Which expression fits best?

1. Thank God I haven't got to *get up* early tomorrow.
2. You'll get a better view of the match if you *stand up*.
3. Let's *rise* to welcome the President.
4. Early to bed and early to *rise* makes a man healthy, wealthy and wise.

JOKE YOUR WAY round trouble spots

1. How to make a speech: *Stand up*, speak up, shut up.
2. Secretary: I *get up* early.
3. My formula for success is *rise / get up* early, work late, and strike oil. PAUL GETTY
4. At the end of a presentation, the chairman *rose / got up* and said, "Your presentation has not left me any the wiser."

12 Bank

TEST YOURSELF : Right or Wrong?

	R	W
1. Several people were fishing from the river *bank*.	✔	
2. I had lost my key and had to sleep on a park ~~bank~~ *bench*.		✔
3. The sun disappeared behind a ~~bench~~ *bank* of clouds.		✔
4. Our boat struck a *sandbank*. One person fell overboard.	✔	

JOKE YOUR WAY round trouble spots

1. My *bank* just sent me a note that my account is overdrawn again. I'm going to try another *bank*. They can't all be overdrawn.
2. A couple walking in the park noticed a young man and woman sitting on a *bench*, kissing passionately.
3. "I fell off the *bench*."

13 bei

TEST YOURSELF : The choice is yours

1. Er nahm das Kind *bei* der Hand.	He took the child *by* the hand.
2. Er hat ein Haus *bei* Berlin.	He has got a house *near* Berlin.
3. Er starb *bei* einem Unfall.	He died *in* an accident.
4. Ich war *bei* meinem Freund.	I was *at* my friend's.

JOKE YOUR WAY round trouble spots

1. A bank is a place where they lend you an umbrella *in* fair weather and ask for it back when it begins to rain.
2. A well-known American movie actress died *in* an accident.
3. I wished to be *near* my mother.
4. A man bought a parrot *at* an auction after some very brisk bidding.

14 bekommen

TEST YOURSELF : Right or Wrong?

	R	W
1. Light colours *become (stehen)* you, Tina.	✔	
2. Tony *became (wurde)* a doctor.	✔	
3. Waiter, can I ~~become~~ *get* a steak?		✔
4. Can you *get* BBC World Service on your radio?	✔	
5. My wife's ~~becoming~~ *having (bekommt)* a baby.		✔
6. She ~~obtained~~ *received* a letter from her ex-friend today.		✔
7. I managed to *obtain / get* the book I wanted.	✔	

JOKE YOUR WAY round trouble spots

1. An Italian prime minister should not think of getting married until he *gets* a steady job.
2. She *became* his step-mother.
3. "Every time I ask someone the time I *receive / get* a different answer."

15 bemerken

TEST YOURSELF : Make the right choice

1. "I'm not my usual self tonight," *remarked* Tom.
   "Yes, I've *noticed* the improvement," said Tina.
2. Did you hear about the policeman who gave out a hundred parking tickets before he *realized* he was at a drive-in movie?

JOKE YOUR WAY round trouble spots

	R	W
1. "Our economics professor talks to himself. Does yours?" "Yes, but he isn't *aware of* it. He thinks we're listening!"		✔
2. Have you ever ~~mentioned~~ *noticed* how England wins the World Cup only under a Labour government?		✔

3. "Doctor, I was looking in the mirror this morning, and I ~~remarked~~ *noticed* that one of my eyes is different from the other!" ✔

16 besonders

TEST YOURSELF : The choice is yours

1. I usually agree with her, but in this *particular* case I think she's wrong.
2. She has her own *special* way of doing things.
3. She took *particular* care not to damage the parcel.
4. You'll need a *special* tool to do that.

JOKE YOUR WAY round trouble spots

1. Scotsman: Could I hire a horse, please?
   Farmer: Certainly, Sir. Any *particular* kind?
2. Sign in bar: We have a *special* arrangement with the bank. They don't serve beer and we don't cash cheques.
3. But one day a gypsy sold her a *special* Chinese love potion for 50 pence – and it worked.

17 besuchen

TEST YOURSELF : Spot the mistakes and correct them

1. His son ~~visits~~ *goes to / attends* a very expensive private school.
2. Let's ~~attend~~ *go to see / watch* a James Bond film tonight.
3. My family ~~goes to see~~ *visits* the British Museum every year.

JOKE YOUR WAY round trouble spots

1. Did you hear about the dog that *visited* a flea circus and stole the show?
2. I *went to see* a lawyer and said ...
3. Which countries did you *visit*?
4. Meetings that you chair are infinitely better than those that you merely *attend*.

18 bis

TEST YOURSELF : What is it in English?

1. Let's wait *until / till* the rain stops.
2. He should have been here *by* one o'clock.
3. May I see you home *as far as* the bus stop?

JOKE YOUR WAY round trouble spots

1. You're not a star *until* they can spell your name in Karachi.
2. Surely everybody has seen a computer without clothes on *by* now.
3. *By the time* a man can read women like a book he's too old to start a library.
4. Concorde travels at twice the speed of sound, which is fun, *except for the fact that* you can't hear the movie *until* two hours after you land.

19 bitte sehr / bitte schön

TEST YOURSELF : How would you react?

1. Another cup of tea?	(Yes), please.
2. May I use your phone?	Go ahead.
3. Have you got an aspirin for me?	Here you are.
4. Thank you for helping me.	You're welcome.

JOKE YOUR WAY round trouble spots

1. "The acoustics in this theatre are fantastic." – "*Pardon*?"
2. "Two martinis, *please*!" – "Dry?" asked the barman. – "No," said the German, "zwei!" The waiter returned, "Two martinis, *here you are*, sir."

20 blamieren

TEST YOURSELF : Match the numbers and the letters

A. 4 sich blamieren	B. 2 jemanden blamieren
C. 3 selbst Schuld sein	D. 1 jemanden beschuldigen

JOKE YOUR WAY round trouble spots

1. "Are you trying to *make a fool out of* me?"
2. "It's nice of you to *take the blame*," his boss said.
3. "Who says (that) *you are to blame*?"

21 brauchen

TEST YOURSELF : Right or Wrong?

		R	W
1.	How long *did it take* you to write this book?	✔	
2.	You *needn't* help me tomorrow.	✔	
3.	He needed / *It took him* an hour to write the letter.		✔
4.	A bank is a place that will lend you money if you can prove that you ~~needn't~~ *don't need / require* it.		✔
5.	I'd like to give you something you ~~are requiring~~ *need* ...		✔

→ MERKE:

- *require* und *need* stehen gewöhnlich nicht in der Verlaufsform
- du musst nicht tun / brauchst nicht zu tun: *You needn't do*
- *Take your time!* Lass dir Zeit!

JOKE YOUR WAY round trouble spots

1. ... he *need not* exist in order to save us.
2. *It takes* a lot of experience for a girl to kiss like a beginner.
3. To err is human, but to really foul things up *requires* a computer.
4. When *it takes him* all night to do what he used to do all night.
5. I *didn't need a* diploma to do what I do.

22 bringen

TEST YOURSELF : The choice is yours

1. Tom had an accident. He was *taken* to hospital.
2. Tina went to see him and *brought* him some flowers.
3. Tom asked her to *take* some letters to the post office for him.
4. A young doctor *took* Tina home in his car.

JOKE YOUR WAY round trouble spots

1. "Waiter! Waiter! You've *brought* me a lobster with just one claw!" ...
   "Okay, then *take* this one away and *bring* me the winner."
2. "When I was seven years old my father *took* me to the zoo."
   "Were you accepted?"
3. Soldier: And what happens if the parachute fails to open?
   Sergeant: *Bring* it back and you'll get another.

23 Chef

TEST YOURSELF : The choice is yours

1. Crazy Horse was a famous *chief* of the Sioux.
2. Our new French *chef* is an excellent cook.
3. The *boss* hates us being late.
4. I'd like to speak to the *manager*. I have a complaint to make.

JOKE YOUR WAY round trouble spots

1. The receptionist stared at the red-skinned guest and asked, "Do you have a reservation, *Chief*?"
2. In the cockpit of a Boeing taking a hundred passengers to their Turkish holiday resort, the *chief pilot* is celebrating his birthday.
3. The only reason my *boss* never says an unkind remark about anyone is because he only ever talks about himself.

24 Daten

TEST YOURSELF : What is it in German?

1.	What's the *date*?	*Datum*
2.	Don't forget to *date* your cheque.	*datieren*
3.	Young people's clothes *date* quickly nowadays.	*veralten*
4.	He's trying to *date* a beauty queen.	*sich verabreden mit*
5.	The *data* is (!) still being analysed.	*Daten*

JOKE YOUR WAY round trouble spots

1. Reliability of *delivery dates* is inversely proportional to the tightness of your company's production schedules.
2. Bisexuality immediately doubles your chances for a *date* on Saturday night.
3. Which of the boys is older?
   The two boys are the same age. In British English the day comes before the month. In American English the month is given first.

25 dezent / diskret

TEST YOURSELF : Match the numbers and the letters

1. C • 2. B • 3. E • 4. A • 5. D

JOKE YOUR WAY round trouble spots

1. It is not the crook in modern business that we fear, but the *decent* man who doesn't know what he is doing.
2. A German businessman entered a Swiss bank. He looked *discreetly* around ...
3. What is the difference between valour and *discretion*?
   To travel on an ocean liner without tipping would be courage. To come back on a different ocean liner would be *discretion.*

26 dick

TEST YOURSELF : Right or Wrong?

	R	W
1. He speaks English with a *thick* accent.	✔	
2. Tina takes slimming pills. She thinks she's too ~~thick~~ *fat*.		✔
3. I hate reading *fat* books.	✔	
4. Tom's a bit *thick* – but don't tell his parents.	✔	

JOKE YOUR WAY round trouble spots

1. There was a boarding house ... where the dust was so *thick* on the floor ...
2. The opera is never over until the *fat* lady sings.
3. Jimmy is so *thick.*

27 diskutieren

TEST YOURSELF : Right or Wrong?

	R	W
1. We discussed ~~about~~ German politics for hours.		✔
2. We had a long *discussion about* German politics.	✔	
3. I said that politics was not what I wanted to *discuss* ~~about~~.		✔

JOKE YOUR WAY round trouble spots

"No *discussions about* salaries with any other member of the staff. It is your own personal business, and you shouldn't go around and *discuss* salaries with your colleagues."

28 eigen

TEST YOURSELF : Complete the sentences

1. *Ich sah es mit eigenen Augen.* I saw it with *my own* eyes.
2. *Ich habe ein eigenes Zimmer.* I've got *my own* room.
3. *Der eigene Sohn des Chefs war der Dieb.* The *boss's own* son was the thief.

JOKE YOUR WAY round trouble spots

1. "At the time of the Flood," replied the Scot, "we the MacNabs, had *a boat of our own.*"
2. Wonderful opportunity for woman to join fishing partners. Must have *her own boat* and be able to cook and wash up.
3. If a politician buys votes with private money, he is a dirty crook; but if he buys them with *the people's own money*, he's a great liberal.

29 entschuldigen

TEST YOURSELF : Is it *excuse me* or *I apologise*?

1. "*Excuse me*, miss. I'm writing a phone book."
2. "Officer," said the Sweet Young Thing coming into the police station, "where do I *apologise* for shooting my husband?"

JOKE YOUR WAY round trouble spots

1. The new secretary to her boss. "*Excuse me*, is 'comma' written with one or two 'm's?"
2. "*I'm sorry* that I didn't come to your birthday party." – "No need *to apologise*," replied his boss. "You were there!"
3. "I'm a self-made man." – "We accept your *apology*."
4. The judge asked, "What possible *excuse* can you have for freeing this defendant?"

30 erinnern

TEST YOURSELF : Spot the mistakes and correct them

1. I can't seem to *remember* your name, and please don't ~~remember~~ *remind* me!
2. By the time you reach 75 years of age you've learnt everything. All you have to do is to try and ~~remind~~ *remember* it.
3. The trouble with telling a good joke is that it always ~~remembers~~ *reminds* the other fellow of a bad one.

JOKE YOUR WAY round trouble spots

1. "Do you *remember* those pills they used to give us in the army to keep our minds off girls?"
2. You're getting old when the only thing you want for your birthday is not to be *reminded* of it.
3. Do you *remember saying* you'd give me £10 for passing my exams?

31 erst

TEST YOURSELF : Welches *only* bedeutet *erst*?

	erst
1. How can I believe in God when *only* last week I got my tongue caught in the roller of an electric typewriter?	✔
2. It's no fun to go to the airline desk to complain about lost luggage *only* to (*nur, um zu*) see that the clerk is wearing your clothes!	
3. And I *only* learned how to drive yesterday!	✔

JOKE YOUR WAY round trouble spots

1. "It's *only* 2003 now."
2. "But *first* get those crazy lions out of there."
3. "And *don't* say 'yes' *until* I've finished."

32 es

TEST YOURSELF : What is it in English?

1. When I do good my boss never remembers. When I do wrong – *he never forgets.*
2. *There is no* great genius without some touch of madness.
3. *There are* lies, damned lies and statistics.
4. Sign in a toilet: Please use the toilet brush. Someone had written beneath: *I tried*, but now I've gone back to using paper.
5. A pessimist is a man who thinks all women are bad. An optimist *hopes so.*

JOKE YOUR WAY round trouble spots

1. "Then why the bloody hell didn't you say *so*?"
2. Some people can cook but *don't (don't do it)*. My wife can't cook but *does.*
3. "I don't *know*. My husband bought the tickets."
4. The absent-minded professor's wife went into his study and said, "Do you *know it* was 28 years ago today that you asked me to marry you?" The professor looked up from his work. "And *did you*?"

33 etwas

TEST YOURSELF : Is it *some(thing)* or *any(thing)*?

1. Can you give me *some* money?
2. Of course, do you want *anything* else?
3. I left *some* money on the table.
4. Do you need *some* more money?
5. If I can do *anything* else for you, let me know.
6. There's *something* interesting on TV tonight.

JOKE YOUR WAY round trouble spots

1. An intellectual is a man who has found *something* more interesting than women.
2. A holiday is *something* you have for two weeks that takes fifty weeks to pay for.
3. "What's all this fuss about plutonium?" said Annette. "How can *anything* named after a Disney character be dangerous?"
4. An expert is a man who is like a eunuch in a harem – he knows all about it but can't do *anything* about it.

34 eventuell

TEST YOURSELF : The choice is yours

1. We have made a plan in order to avoid *possible* difficulties.
2. She *eventually* passed her driving test.
3. Our *eventual* aim is to find a drug against cancer.
4. My company may *possibly* use your service very often.

JOKE YOUR WAY round trouble spots

1. I was crying and crying, and *eventually* I found a policeman who said he would help. I asked him, "Do you think we'll ever be able to find them?" He replied, "*Possibly* / *Maybe*, but there are so many places to hide."
2. Conscience is the inner voice which warns us that someone *may be* looking.
3. *Eventually* she said: "Yes, but what colour are the petals?"

35 fahren

TEST YOURSELF : Is it A or B?

1. We'd better **B.** *go by car* to Munich.
2. If you want to enjoy the beautiful scenery of Sweden **A.** *go* by train.
3. I love **A.** *riding* on top of double-decker buses.
4. My grandmother has never **B.** *gone* by taxi.

JOKE YOUR WAY round trouble spots

1. Did you hear about the Scot who won a holiday for two in Majorca? He *went* by himself twice.
2. Policeman: Lady, you *were doing* 85 miles per hour. I only learned how to *drive* yesterday.
3. One charter flight was so crowded that the pilot *went* by boat.
4. "We went *riding* in one of those rickshaws," he told his wife ...

36 falsch

TEST YOURSELF : wrong or false?

1. Education is the process of throwing *false* pearls before real swine.
2. When you dial the *wrong* number, you never get a busy signal.
3. All good generalizations are *false*, including this one.
4. I finally had an orgasm but my doctor told me it was the *wrong* kind.

JOKE YOUR WAY round trouble spots

1. However, he didn't get a medal because it was a *false* start.
2. Have you heard about the Scotsman who took his wife's *false* teeth to work with him every day to stop her eating between meals?
3. Today I dialled a *wrong* number.

37 Fehler

TEST YOURSELF : Right or Wrong?

	R	W
1. Experience is the name we give our ~~faults~~ *mistakes*.		✔
2. Planning means replacing chance by ~~mistake~~ *error*.		✔
3. To find out a girl's *faults*, praise her to her girlfriends.	✔	
4. A hidden *flaw* will not appear till a machine has passed final inspection.	✔	

JOKE YOUR WAY round trouble spots

1. "There, there," she consoled him "who says it was your *fault*?"
2. All great discoveries are made by *mistake*.
3. The only real *errors* are human *errors*.
4. All sorts of computer *errors* are turning up now.

38 Frau und Mann

TEST YOURSELF : What's the best word for Frau and Mann?

1. If you think *women* are better qualified than *men* to pick the best candidates, look at who they marry.
2. Every married *man* knows that the most perfect *husband* in the world belongs to the *woman* next door.
3. A pedestrian is a *man* with two cars, a *wife*, and a son.

JOKE YOUR WAY round trouble spots

1. Two business*men were* having lunch one day when two *women* entered the restaurant. "Let's go," said one. "My *wife* and my lover have just walked in."
2. No *woman* has ever shot her *husband* while he was doing the dishes.
3. A lawyer is addressing a *male* jury, "*Gentlemen*, shall we cast this beautiful young *lady* into a dark, dim cell, ..."
4. The coach of the Chinese *female* Olympic swimming team goes by the name of Do-Ping.

39 fremd

TEST YOURSELF : Which word fits best?

1. In some countries *foreigners* are not allowed to own land.
2. Sorry, I'm a *stranger* here myself.
3. Some people think *alien* influences threaten their way of life.
4. The man in front was a complete *stranger* to him.

JOKE YOUR WAY round trouble spots

1. The softer the currency in a *foreign* country is, the harder the toilet paper.
2. Last week we found out that the woman who'd been sitting watching TV with us for the past eight years was a complete *stranger*.
3. My definition of a *foreigner* is someone who doesn't understand cricket.

40 früher

TEST YOURSELF : What is it in English?

1. I *used to* live in the *former* GDR.
2. Look! Over there is your *former* boss.
3. I'm the new owner. The *previous* owner has died.

JOKE YOUR WAY round trouble spots

1. Dolly asked Priscilla why she had given up her *previous* boyfriend.
2. Boss: You look like a shadow of your *former* self, Tina.
3. I *used to* suffer from a split personality, Doc, ...
4. I *used to be* a werewolf, but I'm all right noooooooow!

41 ganz

TEST YOURSELF : The choice is yours

1. She wasn't telling the *whole* truth.
2. This is *quite* a different problem.
3. The film was *pretty* good.
4. I felt like a *complete* idiot.

JOKE YOUR WAY round trouble spots

1. You have to get to church *pretty / quite* early to get a seat in the back row.
2. Advertising is the art of making *whole lies* out of half truths.
3. You spend *all the time* hitting boards. And when was the last time you were attacked by a piece of wood?
4. I've been collecting compliments *all my life*. Yours is the third.
5. I said to my son, "Finish up *all your* meat and you'll grow up to be just like Daddy." Since then he has only eaten vegetables.

42 geboren

TEST YOURSELF : Right or Wrong?

	R	W
1. ~~She is a born~~ Her *maiden name is* Müller.		✔
2. I *was born* in Berlin.	✔	
3. He is ~~a born~~ German *by birth*.		✔
4. Tom is a *born* businessman.	✔	
5. ~~I have~~ *It's my birthday* today.		✔

JOKE YOUR WAY round trouble spots

1. "Why do you say George is a *born boss*?" – "Because his father owns the business."
2. *It's my wife's birthday tomorrow*. My present will be a real surprise for her. I'm getting her a toaster. She's expecting a Mercedes.
3. "Why were you *born* in Dublin?" – "I wanted to be near my mother."

43 gehen

TEST YOURSELF : What is it in English?

1. *Die Busse nach X gehen stündlich.*	Buses to X *run* every hour.
2. *Das Baby lernt gerade gehen.*	The baby is just learning to *walk*.
3. *Wie geht's deinem Bruder?*	How *is* your brother?
4. *Deine Uhr geht falsch.*	Your watch *is* wrong.

JOKE YOUR WAY round trouble spots

1. Father: Why don't you *walk* around the block?
2. For every successful man, you'll find somebody who says, "I *went* to school with him."
3. If you can *walk* around it, it is a sculpture.
4. And there was this good-looking East Friesian who *went* surf riding. His horse drowned.
5. Sticker on a Mini: This was a Rolls before it *went* through a car wash.
6. God would never have given us the bicycle if he had wanted us to *walk*.

44 genial, Genie

TEST YOURSELF : There are 2 mistakes. Can you find them?

1. The genie granted him three wishes.
2. That was a ~~genial~~ *brilliant* idea.
3. Tom is an undiscovered ~~genie~~ *genius*.
4. Her idea was a stroke of genius.
5. A good genius / genie helped him.

JOKE YOUR WAY round trouble spots

1. Student: I've just had a *brilliant* idea.
2. The guy who invented the first wheel was an idiot, but the guy who invented the other three, now he was *a genius*.

3. A company is *an ingenious* device for obtaining individual profit without individual responsibility.

45 glauben

TEST YOURSELF : think or believe?

1. *Glaubst du, dass sie kommen?*	Do you *think* they'll come?
2. *Ich habe seine Lügen geglaubt.*	I *believed* his lies.
3. *Ich glaube kein Wort davon.*	I don't *believe* a word of it.
4. *Ich glaube, ich habe etwas gehört.*	I *thought* I heard a noise.

JOKE YOUR WAY round trouble spots

1. He *thinks* that electricity was invented by Voltaire.
2. Of course I *believe* in luck.
3. Since a politician never *believes* what he says, he is always astonished when others do.
4. An optimist *thinks* the glass is half full. The pessimist *thinks* it's half empty.
5. "Do you really *believe* in free love?"

46 gleich

TEST YOURSELF : What is it in English?

1. There is *an equal* number of boys and girls in the class.
2. My sister and I do not *look alike.*
3. I bought the *same* car as you.
4. They tried to treat all their children *alike.*
5. *It doesn't matter to me* what you do.

JOKE YOUR WAY round trouble spots

1. In our company all colleagues are *equal*, only the salaries aren't.
2. A woman advertised for a husband. The following day she got fifty replies, all saying the *same* thing: "You can have mine."
3. If I had my life to live over again, I'd start making the *same* mistakes earlier.
4. Wife: It says here that marriage makes people look *alike* and I know that I'm beginning to talk like you.

47 Glück

TEST YOURSELF : Right or Wrong?

		R	W
1.	You don't look very *happy* today.	✔	
2.	I was nearly killed in an accident and I know I'm ~~happy~~ *lucky* to be alive.		✔
3.	We wish her good ~~happiness~~ *luck* in her new career.		✔
4.	Their children are a constant source of *happiness.*	✔	

JOKE YOUR WAY round trouble spots

1. Tom is *lucky*. He has got a wife and a car, and they both work.
2. Best wishes for a *happy* and successful first marriage.
3. Amusement is the *happiness* of those who cannot think.
4. Success is just a matter of *luck*. Ask a failure.

48 groß

TEST YOURSELF : Which word fits the context best?

1. Time may be a *great* healer, but it's a lousy beautician.
2. If only God would give me a clear sign! Like making a *large* deposit in my name at a Swiss bank.
3. If your company is *big* enough, your mistakes become standards.

JOKE YOUR WAY round trouble spots

1. A small thing can be made *large* by the right kind of advertising.
2. All *great* discoveries are made by mistake.
3. "One thing I really grant you Brits. Your grasshoppers are really a lot *bigger* than ours back in Texas."
4. The giant redwood trees in the USA are *so tall* that squirrels have to wear oxygen masks to collect nuts.

49 gut

TEST YOURSELF : Right or Wrong?

		R	W
1.	A *good* plan today is better than a perfect plan tomorrow.	✔	
2.	If you want to eat ~~good~~ *well* in England, eat three breakfasts.		✔
3.	I bet on a *good* horse today. It took eleven other horses to beat him.	✔	

JOKE YOUR WAY round trouble spots

1. I think if I have a *good* breakfast I can go without food for the rest of the day. I think that until about lunchtime.
2. One door-to-door salesman does very *well* ...
3. Great Caesar's bust is on the shelf,
   And I don't feel so *well* myself.

50 haben

TEST YOURSELF : Is it A, B or C?

1. Hypochondria is the one disease **B.** *I haven't got* / **C.** *I don't have.*
2. Why do some Germans envy the Chinese? – Because they **A.** *have still got* / **C.** *still have* their Wall.
3. The telephone will ring when **A.** *you are having* a shower. You will reach it just in time to hear the click of the caller hanging up.

JOKE YOUR WAY round trouble spots

1. I asked her if she liked Le Corbusier and she replied, "I'd love some – with a little lemon juice in it, if you*'ve got* / you *have any.*"
2. You can fool 88 % of the public all the time, the rest *haven't got / don't have* any money.
3. There are only two specimens of a Neanderthal's head in existence. The British Museum *has (got)* one and Bill *has (got)* the other.

51 halten

TEST YOURSELF : Is it *hold* or *keep*?

1. Here's a five dollar bill – please *keep* the change.
2. The police were unable to *hold* back the crowd.
3. Who *holds* the world record for the long jump?
4. We are not allowed to *keep* dogs in our house.

JOKE YOUR WAY round trouble spots

1. There are two things that are more difficult than *making* an after-dinner speech ...
2. They're letting me *keep* my mother.
3. Sometimes you can make a very effective statement by *holding* your tongue.

4. Well, money isn't everything in life, but it does *keep* you in touch with your children.
5. "I'm only *holding* it."
6. "What do you *think* of our new boss?"

52 handeln

TEST YOURSELF : What is it?

1. He said he wasn't prepared to *bargain* over the price.
2. The company *trades / deals* in computer software.
3. A new man was appointed to *handle* the crisis.
4. Her poems often *deal with* the subject of death.

JOKE YOUR WAY round trouble spots

1. Men and nations will *act* rationally when all other possibilities have been exhausted.
2. A *bargain* is something you buy that is cheaper than something you really need.
3. *Dealing / Trading* in antiques is a strange way to make a living.

53 Hausarbeit

TEST YOURSELF : Is it A, B or C?

1.	work that you do to prepare for something	**B.** *homework*
2.	work for a business that is done by people at home	**A.** *outwork*
3.	work given by teachers for students to do at home	**B.** *homework*
4.	cleaning, making the beds, cooking	**C.** *housework*

JOKE YOUR WAY round trouble spots

1. Pupil: Good, because I haven't done my *homework.*
2. "*Housework*, it's so boring," said the bride.
3. "Well, how the hell can I help you if you don't do your *homework*?"

54 hören

TEST YOURSELF : Right or Wrong?

	R	W
1. I like to ~~hear~~ *listen to* classical music.		✔
2. Although we *listened* carefully, we couldn't *hear* a word of what they were saying.	✔	
3. ~~Hear~~ *Listen*! Somebody is knocking at the door.		✔
4. We hope to *hear* from you soon.	✔	
5. She was shouting something we couldn't ~~listen~~ *hear* very well.		✔

JOKE YOUR WAY round trouble spots

1. If you want your wife to *listen*, then talk to another woman.
2. "Yes, I can *hear* you distinctly."
3. I *hear* you are going into hospital next week for a brain operation – the doctors hope to give you one.
4. There are only two kinds of executives who fail: those who *listen to* nobody, and those who *listen to* everybody.

55 ja

TEST YOURSELF : Match the numbers and the letters

1. C. **2. D.** **3. A.** **4. B.**

1.	You are coming along, aren't you?	**C.**	Yes, of course.
2.	Can we trust him?	**D.**	Yes, completely.
3.	Would you like another drink?	**A.**	Yes, I'd love one.
4.	Excuse me, sir.	**B.**	Yes?

JOKE YOUR WAY round trouble spots

1. "Why, McGregor," said the doctor, "you have lost your stutter!"
   "*Yes, I have*," said McGregor ...
2. Young secretary: *Yes, but* it takes me longer.
3. "Did you give your wife a lecture on economy like I told you?"
   "*Yes, (of course) I did / I (certainly) did.*"

56 jede(r/s)

TEST YOURSELF : Right or Wrong?

		R	W
1.	There are two sides to ~~each~~ *every* argument until you take one.		✔
2.	~~Each~~ *Any* fool can make a rule.		✔
3.	The law protects *everybody* who is able to afford a lawyer.	✔	
4.	Did you hear about the Irish millionaire? He ordered two chinchillas for his wife. One for ~~every~~ *each* chin.		✔

JOKE YOUR WAY round trouble spots

1. He has been invited to *every* great party in town ... once.
2. "That'll be five dollars *each*."
3. *Any* club that would accept me as a member, I wouldn't want to join.
4. "I noticed one thing about him – he seemed to dress better *each* time."

57 Karte

TEST YOURSELF : Right or Wrong?

		R	W
1.	They never taught us how to read a ~~card~~ *map* at school.		✔
2.	She sent me a lovely *card* on my birthday.	✔	
3.	The documents are in my ~~map~~ *briefcase / folder*. But I left it at the office.		✔
4.	Sorry, I can't play *cards* this evening; we've got ~~cards~~ *tickets* for the theatre.		✔

JOKE YOUR WAY round trouble spots

1. He thought it was a *map* of the Sahara Desert.
2. "I don't know. My husband bought the *tickets*."
3. A man on holiday in Italy sent a *card* to his psychiatrist. It read: "Having a wonderful time. Why?"

58 klein

TEST YOURSELF : Which word fits best?

1. The floor was covered in *tiny* bits of paper.
2. You'll always be Daddy's *little* girl.

3. There may be some *minor* changes to our plan.
4. That dress is too *small* for me.
5. He is *smaller* than me.

JOKE YOUR WAY round trouble spots

1. Our farm is so *small* that the cows have to produce condensed milk.
2. A *little* girl asked her father, "Daddy, before you married Mommy, who told you how to drive?"
3. "Listen boys! When the enemy is only 200 metres away you may start retreating. Being a *little* lame, I'll leave now."
4. Inflation is when wallets are getting bigger and shopping bags *smaller.*
5. The disadvantage of being the world's *shortest* person is that you are the last person to know when it's raining.

59 kochen

TEST YOURSELF : Right or Wrong?

	R	W
1. Shall I ~~cook~~ *make* you some coffee?		✔
2. Shall I *boil* or fry the eggs?	✔	
3. The milk has ~~cooked~~ *boiled* over!		✔
4. I'll ~~boil~~ *make* you some soup.		✔

JOKE YOUR WAY round trouble spots

1. The new husband sat down at the table after his young bride had just *cooked* her first chicken ...
2. "I am sorry, Mr Jones, there isn't much I can do. Well, perhaps I could *boil* you an egg."

60 kontrollieren

TEST YOURSELF

1. The army used terror to *control* the people.
2. Our tickets were *checked* twice on the S-Bahn.
3. Please *check* the oil and water before setting off.
4. He was finding it difficult to *control* his feelings.

JOKE YOUR WAY round trouble spots

1. Old Jake went for his annual *medical check-up.*
2. In my house there's this light switch that doesn't do anything. Every so often I would flick it on and off just to *check.*
3. *Self-control* is when you go into a supermarket to buy a pint of milk and all you buy is a pint of milk.

61 krank

TEST YOURSELF : Is it A or B?

1. Bad luck! Poor Anne fell **(B.)** *ill* on holiday.
2. Her husband thought she was a very **(A.)** *sick* woman.
3. But I don't think she was seriously **(B.)** *ill.*

JOKE YOUR WAY round trouble spots

1. I'm losing faith in my doctor. All his patients seem to be *ill.*
2. What does one send to a *sick* florist?
3. The art of medicine consists in amusing the patient while Nature cures the *disease.*
4. "... every time Liverpool is playing at home mid-week you ask permission to go and visit your grandmother who's seriously *ill.*" ... "You don't think, by any chance, she's pretending to be *ill*?"

62 kurz, kürzlich, vor kurzem

TEST YOURSELF : The choice is yours

1. I haven't seen them *recently / lately.*
2. She arrived *shortly* after us.
3. She met John *briefly* on Friday night.
4. I saw him *shortly* before he died.
5. We received a letter from him *recently / lately.*
6. Tell me *briefly* what your story is about.

JOKE YOUR WAY round trouble spots

1. "I've been telephoning Australia *recently / lately.*"
2. *Shortly after* the stewardess has served the coffee, the airplane encounters turbulence.
3. *Shortly before* the plate reached them, one of the Scotsmen fainted ...
4. Student: I think so, unless he wrote something *recently / lately.*

63 lassen

TEST YOURSELF : Right or Wrong?

	R	W
1. *Let* me answer your question.	✔	
2. Why don't you ~~let~~ *have* your hair cut?		✔
3. We ~~leave~~ *let* the children play in our garden.		✔
4. We *made* him repeat the whole story.	✔	
5. ~~Let~~ *Leave* father alone, please. He's very tired.		✔

JOKE YOUR WAY round trouble spots

1. "I can't read, I can't write, and the teacher won't even *let* me talk."
2. On holiday, people drive thousands of miles just to *have* their picture taken in front of their cars.
3. Anne: Dad, *let* me take my driving test. I'm old enough now.
4. "He not only lied about the size of his yacht. He made me row."
5. Just *leave* the most difficult problems for the laziest managers to solve.

64 leben

TEST YOURSELF : It's going to be difficult

1. Where do you *live*? – I'm still *living* at my mother's at the moment.
2. Is your father still *alive*?
3. My father shows a *lively* interest in politics.
4. Don't spend your whole *life* worrying about money.
5. He risked his *life* to save the *lives* of his neighbours.

JOKE YOUR WAY round trouble spots

1. God is not dead, but *alive* ...
2. Jesus *lives*. Does this mean we won't get an Easter holiday then?
3. The main difference between Los Angeles and yoghurt is that yoghurt has an active *living* culture.
4. "Waiter, there's a dead fly in my soup!"
   "What do you expect for 50p, *a live one*?"
5. The cardinal rule of politics – never get caught in bed with a *live* man or a dead woman.

65 leicht

TEST YOURSELF : The choice is yours

1. He didn't make it *easy* for me to leave.
2. I woke up with a *slight* headache.
3. Modern video cameras are *light* and *easy* to carry.

JOKE YOUR WAY round trouble spots

1. He has a *slight* problem with the future.
2. It's *easy* to be a humorist when you have the whole government working for you.
3. "*Easy*," the millionaire replied. "I told her I was 95."
4. Tom: And that will make it *lighter*?

66 leihen

TEST YOURSELF : Tricky translations

1. Can I *borrow* your car?
2. Can you *lend* me your car?
3. He *borrowed* a car from his friend.
4. He *lent* me his car.

JOKE YOUR WAY round trouble spots

1. A consultant is someone who *borrows* your watch to tell you what time it is and then walks away with it.
2. A banker is a fellow who *lends* you his umbrella when the sun is shining and wants it back the minute it begins to rain.
3. Always *borrow* money from a pessimist. He doesn't expect to get it back.

67 letzte

TEST YOURSELF : Where do these words fit?

1. When did you *last* see Tom Paxton?
2. I saw him when he read from his *latest* novel.
3. He said he'd arrive by 10 o'clock *at the latest.*
4. I wouldn't marry you if you were the *last* person on earth.

JOKE YOUR WAY round trouble spots

1. The *latest* kind of computer was presented at Cebit in Hannover.
2. "Nonsense! That's the *last* thing you'd do."
3. According to the *latest* statistics, there are three million Americans who aren't working.

68 liegen, legen, lügen

TEST YOURSELF : Right or Wrong?

	R	W
1. He ~~lay~~ *laid* the money on the table.		✔
2. Then he ~~laid~~ *lay* down on the sofa.		✔
3. He had been *lying* to the police about the money.	✔	
4. His cat was ~~lieing~~ *lying* fast asleep by the fire.		✔

JOKE YOUR WAY round trouble spots

1. Cannes is where you *lie* on the beach and look at the stars – or vice versa.
2. "Don't blame me. I only *lay* the table."
3. First wife: Does your husband *lie* awake all night?
   Second wife: Yes, and he *lies* in his sleep, too.
4. Here *lies* a poet – where's the great surprise!
   Since all men know, a poet deals in *lies*.

69 lustig

TEST YOURSELF : Is it A or B?

1. It's **A.** *no fun* being a boss. You have to come in early to see who comes in late.
2. It is **B.** *funny* (= strange) how a wife can spot a blonde hair on a chap's coat, yet miss the garage doors.
3. You're not yourself today. Have **A.** *fun* (= enjoy yourself) while you can.
4. Everything is **B.** *funny* as long as it happens to somebody else.

JOKE YOUR WAY round trouble spots

1. *It's no fun* to go to the airline desk to complain about lost luggage only to see the clerk wearing your clothes!
2. "No need to be sarcastic," said the wife, "*it's not* at all *funny*." – "I'm not trying to *be funny*," he said, "I've left the tickets on the piano."
3. "I didn't come here to *be made fun of*."

70 machen

TEST YOURSELF : What is it in English?

1. Sie *macht* ihre eigenen Kleider. — She *makes* her own clothes.
2. Er *macht* viele Überstunden. — He *does* a lot of overtime.
3. Ich *mache* dir eine Tasse Tee. — I'll *make* you a cup of tea.
4. Tom *macht* heute sein Examen. — Tom *is doing* his exam today.
5. Ich *mache* etwa 20 Reisen im Jahr. — I *make* about 20 trips a year.

JOKE YOUR WAY round trouble spots

1. I *took* a speed reading course and read War And Peace in twenty minutes. It's about Russia.
2. In six days God *made* Heaven and Earth, the Sea and all that is in them – he was self-employed.
3. "Waiter! Waiter! What is this fly *doing* in my soup?"
4. Honeymoon is the holiday a man *takes* before beginning work under a new boss.
5. Anybody who can still *do* at seventy what he was *doing* at twenty wasn't *doing* much at twenty.

71 meinen

TEST YOURSELF : What is it in English?

1. Have you ever been to a zoo? I *mean* as a visitor?
2. If you *think* nothing is impossible, try getting your name off a mailing list.
3. He's a guy who can say absolutely nothing and *mean* it.

JOKE YOUR WAY round trouble spots

1. Just when you *think* you've got the promotion in the bag, some new guy will come along and marry the boss's daughter.
2. "I wonder what he *meant* by that," worried the other.
3. Boss: What do you *mean* you *think* ...
4. If God had *meant* us *to* be homosexuals, he would have created Adam and Eric.

72 die meisten

TEST YOURSELF : Right or Wrong?

	R	W
1. ~~The most~~ *Most* people in our village are farmers.		✔
2. *The most* important thing in life is happiness.	✔	
3. The rain in Spain stays ~~most~~ *mostly* in the plains.		✔
4. It's *most* kind of you to invite me to your party.	✔	

JOKE YOUR WAY round trouble spots

1. Selling is *the most* exciting thing you can do with your clothes on.
2. A conservative is a man who thinks and sits, *mostly* sits.
3. Pauline: That's a change! *Most* young men want me to say 'yes'.
4. Ronald: Yes, doctor, I spill *most* of it.

73 Mensch

TEST YOURSELF : What is it in English?

1. An alcoholic is a *person* who drinks more than his doctor.
2. Two *people* getting together to write a book is like three *people* getting together to have a baby. One of them is superfluous.
3. A zoo is a place devised for animals to study the behaviour *of human beings.*
4. Our neighbours are nice *people.* They listen to us attentively – through a wall.

JOKE YOUR WAY round trouble spots

1. Mother: Helen, what kind of a *person* is your new friend?
2. If a politician ... tries to buy them with the *people's* own money, he's a great liberal.
3. If you want to make a *man* very angry, tell him you are going to pray for him.
4. Doesn't it make you feel a little insecure to know that if you're a *human being,* your body is worth 98 cents?

74 müssen

TEST YOURSELF : What is it in English?

1. "Do you serve women in this bar?" – "No, sir, you *have to* bring your own."
2. If you like laws and sausages, you *must not* watch either of them being made.
3. It's the final proof of God's omnipotence that he *need not* exist in order to save us.

JOKE YOUR WAY round trouble spots

1. There are two kinds of men: those we may dream about and those we *must* marry.
2. I *needn't* tell my wife anything. My neighbours do it for me.
3. An Italian prime minister *mustn't* think of getting married until he gets a steady job.
4. "You will *have to* cut out drinking, smoking and sex."

75 Nachricht

TEST YOURSELF : Right or Wrong?

	R	W
1. What's the latest ~~message~~ *news* about the terrorist attack?		✔
2. That's an interesting piece of news.	✔	
3. Eight o'clock! Can you put the *news* on?	✔	
4. ~~These are~~ *This is* bad news.		✔
5. Excuse me; is there a ~~news~~ *message* for me?		✔

JOKE YOUR WAY round trouble spots

1. "Here's *some good news*," announced Radio Eriwan, "Lenin's mother is still alive. Now *the bad news*: she's pregnant."
2. I think my beeper is a little too powerful. Every time I get *a message*, my garage door opens.
3. "I have *some good news* and *some bad news* for you. First of all, you'll never be able to work again." My uncle said, "Okay, now what's *the bad news*?"
4. "Leave *a message* at the beep, and we'll get back to you as soon as possible."

76 nahe, nächst

TEST YOURSELF : The choice is yours

1. Where's the *nearest* toilet?
2. Turn left at the *next* traffic lights.
3. Tom is a *close* relative of our headmaster.
4. I'd like to sit *near* the window.

JOKE YOUR WAY round trouble spots

1. I got the prize for being *closest*.
2. "I wanted to be *near* my mother."
3. Asked what his favourite drink was, he replied "the next one."

77 paar

TEST YOURSELF : The choice is yours

1. Doctor, I keep thinking I'm a *pair* of curtains.
2. I flew over on Concorde. That plane is so fast it gives you an extra *couple* of hours to look for your luggage.
3. Customer: I'm looking for a *pair* of alligator shoes.

JOKE YOUR WAY round trouble spots

1. "Try riding a bike a *few* miles every day."
2. I would like to buy a *pair* of shorts to wear around my gymnasium.
3. At a party a *couple* was discussing the difficulties of family budgets.

78 passen

TEST YOURSELF : Right or Wrong?

	R	W
1. I work part time, which ~~fits~~ *suits* me fine.		✔
2. He ~~suits~~ *matches* the description of the bank robber.		✔
3. The book is small enough to *fit* in your pocket.	✔	

JOKE YOUR WAY round trouble spots

1. She's got a memory like an elephant and a shape to *match.*
2. Bob: I really like your suit. It *fits* you like a glove.
   Ron: That's the trouble. It should *fit* me like a suit.
3. The tall blonde told the assistant in the fashion shop that she wanted a pair of low heels. – "To *go with* what, madam?"

79 Pause

TEST YOURSELF : Which word fits best?

1. We decided to take a short *break.*
2. At school kids have *break* in Britain or *recess* in the USA.
3. After a *pause,* she said 'Yes.'
4. Can we stop for a minute? I've got a headache. I need a *rest.*

JOKE YOUR WAY round trouble spots

1. "I just took my *coffee break* before I came in."
2. God created the world in six days. On the seventh day, He had a *rest*. On the eighth day, He started getting complaints.

80 Pension

TEST YOURSELF : Fill in the blanks

1. At the *boarding house / guest house* I stayed in, they changed the sheets every week. From one room to another.
2. Tom has to live on a small *pension*.
3. We all wish you a long and happy *retirement.*

JOKE YOUR WAY round trouble spots

1. Have you noticed how every prominent politician, even former prime ministers, decide to write books when they *retire*?
2. "How long do you want them?" – "I want to buy them, not to *rent* them."

81 Platz

TEST YOURSELF : What is it in English?

1. Please *take the seat* next to me.
2. *Make room* for the President and his wife.
3. I'd like a window *seat.*
4. Is there enough *space* for my suitcase?

JOKE YOUR WAY round trouble spots

1. The *space* between her breasts was called Silicon Valley.
2. You have to get to church pretty early to get a *seat / place* in the back row.
3. God isn't dead; he just couldn't find a *parking space.*
4. He heard that most accidents *take place* within five miles of the home, so he moved.
5. Yes. I also noticed that a lot of people left to make *room / space* for it.

82 Politik

TEST YOURSELF : Right or Wrong?

		R	W
1.	Let's not talk about *politics* now.	✔	
2.	What is the party's ~~politics~~ *policy* on immigration?		✔
3.	Honesty is the best ~~politic~~ *policy.*		✔
4.	Read your *policy* very carefully before you sign it.	✔	

JOKE YOUR WAY ROUND trouble spots

1. A *politician* is a person with whose *politics* we don't agree ...
2. Mrs Smith had two grown-up sons. One went into *politics* and the other is a nice, hard-working boy.
3. An insurance salesman was trying to sell a *policy* to a factory owner.

83 Preis

TEST YOURSELF : Right or Wrong?

		R	W
1.	It's terrible bringing up a family today, considering the *price* of beer and cigarettes.	✔	
2.	I really don't deserve this ~~price~~ *prize*. But then, I've got arthritis and I didn't deserve that either.		✔
3.	If there is ever a ~~prize~~ *price* on your head take it.		✔

JOKE YOUR WAY round trouble spots

1. How do you double the *price* of a Trabi? – Fill up the petrol tank.
2. Steve has been awarded first *prize* ...

84 Profit

TEST YOURSELF : What is it in English?

1. An accountant is a man whom we hire to explain to the tax authorities that we haven't made the *profit* they think we have.
2. There isn't much *profit* in running a restaurant these days.
3. The new sports centre will bring lasting *benefit* to the community.

JOKE YOUR WAY round trouble spots

1. It's a socialist idea that making *profits* is a vice; I consider the real vice is making losses.
2. How to be insulting: I wish I had a lower IQ, so I could *benefit* from your conversation.
3. Manager: No problem. We *profit* from repairing them.

85 Prozess

TEST YOURSELF : What is it in English?

1. Reforming the education system will be a slow *process.*
2. He won the *court case* and was awarded damages.
3. She is awaiting *trial* on corruption charges.

JOKE YOUR WAY round trouble spots

1. McTavish was accused of having embezzled a large sum of money. "Not guilty," said the judge after a lengthy *trial.*
2. "In *process*" means that somebody's working on it somewhere.
3. A man was taken to *court* for speeding and went before the judge.
4. My lawyer is beyond brilliant. In a recent *case,* he told his client, "Don't worry. The judge is my cousin ..."

86 Reise

TEST YOURSELF : Right or Wrong?	R	W
1. Who wrote Gulliver's *Travels*?	✔	
2. I booked a ~~journey~~ *voyage* on the Queen Mary.		✔
3. We went on a day *trip* to the mountains.	✔	
4. The Titanic sank on its first *voyage.*	✔	
5. They went on a long train ~~trip~~ *journey* across India.		✔
6. I am ~~travelling~~ *going* to Italy on Monday.		✔

JOKE YOUR WAY round trouble spots

1. A guide on a conducted *tour* of Italy ...
2. I took a weekend *trip* to Istanbul last week.
3. "Just one more thing – cancelling my *voyage* on the Titanic."

87 Rezept

TEST YOURSELF : Right or Wrong ?

		R	W
1.	The doctor gave me a ~~reception~~ *prescription* for antibiotics.		✔
2.	What's her *recipe* for success?	✔	
3.	There's no *prescription* for happiness.	✔	
4.	His latest book met with a mixed ~~receipt~~ *reception.*		✔

JOKE YOUR WAY round trouble spots

1. Opening line for public speakers: After such a warm *reception* I can hardly wait to hear myself speak.
2. A *recipe* in a Scottish cookbook: First, you borrow a pot ...
3. "I'll give you a *prescription* for some sleeping pills," says the doctor.
4. The director was looking over the expense accounts of the sales department. "What are these *receipts* here?" he asked his sales manager.

88 richtig

TEST YOURSELF : Which is the best word for *richtig*?

1. Is that a *real* diamond?
2. I hope we're doing the *right* thing.
3. You should do your homework *properly.*
4. If my calculations are *correct*, we should arrive in 15 minutes.

JOKE YOUR WAY round trouble spots

1. My birthday gift to my wife will be a *real* surprise for her.
2. You know your house isn't *properly* insulated when you have to put snow tires on your vacuum cleaner.
3. French politicians say, "We want Britain to take her *proper* place in Europe," and they mean, "somewhere behind Albania or Bulgaria."
4. An ex-president was asked whether he thought it was *right* for a man of his seventy-five years to be president.

89 ruhig

TEST YOURSELF : Which word fits best?

1. I was looking forward to a *quiet* holiday by the sea.
2. We found a *quiet* town where time seemed to stand *still.*
3. The sea was *calm* when we arrived there.
4. A group of *silent* onlookers was watching our arrival.

JOKE YOUR WAY round trouble spots

1. "This car," said the salesman, "runs so *quietly* you can't hear it, so perfectly you can't smell it and so fast you can't see it."
2. In the supermarket a gentleman was pushing a pram with a screaming boy. He tried to *calm him down* repeating phrases like, "Don't get excited, Albert. Albert, don't yell! Do keep *calm*, Albert." A woman standing next to him said, "It's fantastic how you look after little Albert." The man turned round and said *quietly*, "Madam, I am Albert."

90 Sache

TEST YOURSELF : What is it in English?

1. Pack your *things* for the trip tomorrow.
2. He gave all his money to a humanitarian *cause.*
3. It's a private *matter.*
4. I'll come straight to the *point*: we need more money.

JOKE YOUR WAY round trouble spots

1. Whenever the *cause* of the people is entrusted to professors, it is lost.
2. Success is just a *matter* of luck. Ask a failure.
3. I have come to the conclusion that politics is too serious a *matter* to be left to the politicians.
4. Englishmen hate two *things*: racial discrimination and Irishmen.
5. Only when the final draft of the document has been typed up and printed will the boss remember some important *points* that must be added to the middle of it.

91 sagen

TEST YOURSELF : Right or Wrong?

	R	W
1. Tact is thinking all you say without ~~telling~~ *saying* all you think.		✔
2. Some people have tact and others ~~say~~ *tell* the truth.		✔
3. A diplomat is a man who can *tell* you to go to hell in such a way that you actually look forward to the trip.	✔	

JOKE YOUR WAY round trouble spots

1. "You look worried. What did the doctor *say*?"
   "He *told* me to take these pills for the rest of my life."
2. The drunk approached the policeman. "Officer, can you *tell me* where I am?"
3. Do you *say* a prayer before you eat?

92 schön

TEST YOURSELF : Which word fits best?

1. The two of them make a *handsome* couple.
2. You don't have to be young to be *beautiful.*
3. He has a very *pretty* wife.
4. That's a very *handsome* piece of furniture .

JOKE YOUR WAY round trouble spots

1. "I can't believe that John is in hospital. Only yesterday I saw him with a *beautiful* young blonde girl in a French restaurant."
2. A woman said to the mother of a girl: Oh, what a *pretty* little girl. Is your husband *good-looking*?
3. The young man asked the *beautiful* girl to marry him.
4. Fred remarked that this was a very *handsome* reward for a cat.

93 schon

TEST YOURSELF : What is it in English?

1. Hast du *schon* gefrühstückt?	Have you had breakfast *yet*?
2. Ja, ich habe *schon* gefrühstückt.	Yes, I've *already* had breakfast.
3. Geh *noch nicht.*	Don't go *yet.*

JOKE YOUR WAY round trouble spots

1. He *already* knew how many pockets he had.
2. Ron: Sold your house *yet*?
3. Father: Why don't you go for a run around the block?
   Son: Why? I'm *already* here.
4. The realist knows that *before long* he'll have to wash the glass.

94 Schuld

TEST YOURSELF : Which word fits best?

1. The jury has to decide on the defendant's *guilt* or innocence.
2. We were poor but we have never got into *debt.*
3. It was his *fault* that we were late.

JOKE YOUR WAY round trouble spots

1. Sign in the window of a pawnshop: "Come in! Don't be shy! Borrow your way out of *debts*!"
2. Cleaning lady: Don't *blame me*, sir. I have only been here for a week.
3. "Don't worry," a patient told his psychiatrist. "I'll pay every penny I *owe*, or my name isn't Alexander the Great!"

95 schwer

TEST YOURSELF : Correct the two mistakes

1. In the museum visitors' book, under the heading "Reason for visit", someone had written: "~~Hard~~ *Heavy* rain."
2. Just leave the most *difficult* problems for the laziest managers to solve. They will come up with the quickest solutions.
3. Work smarter – not ~~heavier~~ *harder.*

JOKE YOUR WAY round trouble spots

1. "Doctor, doctor! Everybody thinks I'm a liar."
   "Hmmmm! I find this very *hard* to believe."
2. It's *difficult* to get a man to understand something when his salary depends upon his not understanding it.
3. "This letter is too *heavy*. You have to put more stamps on." – "And that will make it lighter?"
4. It's very *hard* to work with my accountant.

96 sehen

TEST YOURSELF : Which word fits best?

1. Tact is the ability to describe others as they *see* themselves.
2. A Trabi makes your average Skoda *look* like a Ferrari.
3. The boss is the only one who *watches* the clock during a coffee break.

JOKE YOUR WAY round trouble spots

1. If you like laws and sausages, you should never *watch* either one being made.
2. "Waiter! Waiter! *Look*! What is this fly doing in my soup?"
   "Hum ... *Looks* like breaststroke, doesn't it?"
3. Policeman: When I *saw* you coming round that bend I thought: Forty-five at least.
   Woman driver: Well, I always *look* older in this hat.
4. "I *saw* him at the swimming pool one day," she said, "and he *looked* so different without his wallet."
5. A small boy was *watching* his Mum do the washing. "Mum, where did you work before you got this job here with us?"

97 seit

TEST YOURSELF : Right or Wrong?

	R	W
1. I have been playing squash ~~since~~ *for* ten years.		✔
2. I've known Joanna *since* she was born.	✔	
3. A doctor to his patient: "I've been giving you medicine for yellow fever ~~since~~ *for* four weeks and now you tell me that you're Chinese."		✔

JOKE YOUR WAY round trouble spots

1. I haven't been so upset *since* Margaret asked me what I wanted to name the baby. Margaret – that's my secretary.
2. We were married successfully *for* four years. Then my wife lost her job.
3. Patient: Aren't these pills habit-forming?
   Doctor: Rubbish, I've been taking them *for* years.
4. "And how long have you believed in reincarnation?"
   "Ever *since* I was a frog."
5. I have been in love with the same woman *for* forty years. If my wife finds out she'll kill me.

98 sicher

TEST YOURSELF : Which word fits best?

1. It's my firm belief that I and the Pope are infallible – although I'm not *certain* about him.
2. Cars made in Britain are absolutely *safe* and reliable; they have been approved to British Standards BS 9966. (But so was the Titanic.)
3. "How long has old Pedro been fishing?" – "I'm not *sure*, but he's the only member of the angling club fishing with a Louis XV rod."

JOKE YOUR WAY round trouble spots

1. Lawyer: Are you *positive / certain* that the defendant is the man who stole your car? Witness: Well, I was until you cross-examined me. Now I'm not *sure* whether I had a car at all.
2. The American West is a place where men are men, but in San Francisco you can never be *sure / certain.*
3. Psychiatrist to patient: "You have nothing to worry about. Anyone who can pay my bills is *certainly* not a failure."
4. Banks are closing by the hundreds today. If you want to rob one, *make sure* you call first to see if it's still open.
5. Old lady to pilot: Please bring us down *safely.*
6. Graffiti: The only *safe* fast breeder is a rabbit.

99 so

TEST YOURSELF : What is it in English?

1. I'm not *so* stupid *as* to believe that.
2. It's *such* a pity that you can't be with us.
3. I've never heard *such* a thing.
4. I wish we had a house *like that.*

JOKE YOUR WAY round trouble spots

1. "Why is your dog staring at me *like that*?"
2. One charter flight was *so* crowded, the pilot went by boat!
3. Boss: How can one person make *so* many mistakes in a single day?
4. He is *such a* bore, even my legs fall asleep when he talks.

100 sollen

TEST YOURSELF : What is it in English?

1. What *shall* we do this weekend?
2. You *should not* drink and drive.
3. You *ought to have* listened to the warnings.
4. It was *meant to* be an apology but it only made her angry.

JOKE YOUR WAY round trouble spots

1. Angry employer: You *should* have been here at nine o'clock.
2. Patient: *Shall* I start at the beginning?
3. Mum: Dad, you'*re supposed* to take Jimmy to the zoo today.
4. The Commandments don't tell you what you *ought to* do: they only put ideas into your head.
5. If man had been *meant to* fly, he would have been born with wings.

101 suchen

TEST YOURSELF : Which phrase for *suchen* fits best?

1. I spent most of the morning *looking for* my passport.
2. He *searched* desperately for something to say.
3. I think it's time we *seek* legal advice.
4. Passengers are regularly *searched* before they board a plane.

JOKE YOUR WAY round trouble spots

1. A theologian is a blind man in a dark room who is *searching for* a black cat which is not there – and he finds it.
2. "Return samples by airmail and *search* the body for orders."
3. A secretary is a young and attractive lady who is paid to learn how to type letters while she is *looking for* a husband.

102 Tasche

TEST YOURSELF : What is it in English?

1. Our boss expects us to pay for the trip out of our own *pockets.*
2. She opened her *bag* and took out her comb.

3. I left my *briefcase* in the office.
4. When is your book coming out *in paperback*?

JOKE YOUR WAY round trouble spots

1. Just when you think you've got the promotion in the *bag*, some new guy will come along and marry the boss's daughter.
2. A fellow says, "In Florida they use alligators to make *handbags*."
3. Then there was the Irishman who refused to buy a *pocket* calculator. He already knew how many *pockets* he had.
4. Inflation is when *wallets* are getting bigger and shopping *bags* smaller.

103 Termin

TEST YOURSELF : Right or Wrong?

	R	W
1. I've got ~~an appointment~~ *a date* with Tina.		✔
2. I'd like to make an *appointment* with your doctor.	✔	
3. Call my secretary and arrange a *date.*	✔	
4. The ~~appointment~~ *deadline* for applications is 30 April.		✔
5. Should we set a *date* for the next meeting?	✔	

JOKE YOUR WAY round trouble spots

1. I had *an appointment* with my doctor this morning.
2. Bisexuality immediately doubles your chances of a *date* on Saturday night.
3. A man called his doctor for *an appointment*. "I'm sorry," said the man, "but I could be dead by then!" – "No problem. If your wife lets us know, we'll cancel *the appointment.*"

104 tragen

TEST YOURSELF : Right or Wrong?

	R	W
1. Police in many countries ~~wear~~ *carry* guns.		✔
2. He can't *bear* to be laughed at.	✔	
3. Do I have to *wear* a tie?	✔	
4. She ~~carries~~ *bears* the responsibility for most of the changes.		✔

JOKE YOUR WAY round trouble spots

1. Our modern world is so full of problems that if Moses came down from Mount Sinai again, the two tablets he'*d be carrying* would be aspirins.
2. A manager is someone who *bears* more responsibility than power.
3. Some Friesians still think that a transistor is a priest who likes *wearing* women's clothes.
4. I put the wrong size of batteries in the beeper that I *wear* on my belt. The first call I got blew my shoes off.

105 übersehen

TEST YOURSELF : Match the numbers and the letters

1.	I seem to have *overlooked* one important fact.	F.
2.	We *looked over* the house again before we decided to rent it.	D.
3.	Our hotel *overlooked* the lake.	A.
4.	I'm not prepared to *overlook* his behaviour.	C.
5.	The government agency *oversees* the airport.	E.
6.	He's *looking over* the photos he'd taken the day before.	B.

JOKE YOUR WAY round trouble spots

1. The garage mechanic *looked over* Ernie's car and said: "If I were you I'd keep the oil and change the car."
2. Seaside landlady: The only rooms we have at the moment *overlook* the sea. They're £5 a night extra.
3. Unruffled, the employee replied, "Well, I can *overlook* one mistake, but not two in a row!"

106 Übung

TEST YOURSELF : What is it in English?

1. She's *practising* for her piano exam.
2. Have you done your piano *exercises* yet?
3. It takes a lot of *practice* to play the violin well.
4. Roll over and repeat the *exercise* on the other leg.

JOKE YOUR WAY round trouble spots

1. It takes a lot of *practice* for a girl to kiss like a beginner.
2. The best way to stay young is eat well, *exercise* and lie about your age.
3. A specialist is a doctor with a smaller *practice* but a bigger yacht.
4. *Practice* makes perfect, but that's no consolation if you are the dentist's first patient.

107 unter

TEST YOURSELF : Right or Wrong?

	R	W
1. Have you looked ~~below~~ *under* the bed?		✔
2. He was *among* the last to leave.	✔	
3. Someone was having a party in the flat ~~under~~ *below.*		✔
4. He dived *below* the surface of the water.	✔	
5. They thought she had married ~~under~~ *beneath* her.		✔

JOKE YOUR WAY round trouble spots

1. *Among* the books with unhappy endings are cheque books.
2. He entered the vet's clinic with a cat *under* his arm. "It's been as sick as a dog," he said.
3. *Under* capitalism man exploits man; *under* socialism the reverse is true.
4. Sign in a lavatory: "Please use the toilet brush." Someone had written *beneath*: "I tried, but now I've gone back to using paper."

108 verdienen

TEST YOURSELF : Spot the mistakes

1. You ~~are deserving~~ *deserve* a rest after all that hard work.
2. All my children are *earning* now.
3. They didn't ~~earn~~ *deserve* to win.
4. She ~~deserved~~ *earned* a living as a part-time secretary.

JOKE YOUR WAY round trouble spots

1. Democracy is a system that ensures that we shall be governed no better than we *deserve.*
2. The income tax authorities have made up a new tax form with only two lines: **1.** How much do you *earn*? **2.** Send it.
3. Lady: Young man, I am going to give you a dollar not because you *deserve* it, but because it pleases me to do so.

109 Versuch

TEST YOURSELF : What is it in English?

1. Many people do not like the idea of *experiments* on animals.
2. It's his fourth *attempt* at breaking the world record.
3. I doubt they'll be able to help but it's worth a *try.*

JOKE YOUR WAY round trouble spots

1. Having had an argument with your boss, any *attempt* to improve relations makes it worse.
2. The ringmaster came over and asked Tom, "Would you like to have a *try*?"
3. In an *attempt* to boost sales, British Airways announced that ... In order to judge the success of this *experiment*, they wrote to all the wives concerned ...

110 wählen, Wahl

TEST YOURSELF : Right or Wrong?

	R	W
1. He hasn't been ~~elected~~ *selected* for the team.		✔
2. How did you ~~choose~~ *vote* at the last election?		✔
3. Over 60% of members ~~elected~~ *voted* in favour of the candidate.		✔
4. There are plenty of restaurants to *choose* from.	✔	

JOKE YOUR WAY round trouble spots

1. In any organisation it is more important to *select* your enemies than it is to *select* your friends.
2. If *voting* changed anything, they'd make it illegal.
3. A jury consists of twelve persons *chosen / selected* to decide who has the better lawyer.
4. Why did God give all the oil to the Arabs and all the kangaroos to the Australians? – Well, the Australians had first *choice.*

111 während

TEST YOURSELF : What is it in English?

1. I only saw her once *during* my stay in Rome.
2. We repair your car *while* you wait.
3. *During* the summer season, all the hotels are full.
4. You can go swimming *while* I'm having lunch.

JOKE YOUR WAY round trouble spots

1. *During* the dance the blonde says to her partner, "I'm dancing a tango, and you?"
2. No woman has ever shot her husband *while* he was doing the dishes.
3. Honeymoon is the period *during* which the bride trusts the bridegroom's word of honour.
4. There were four wise men. *While* following the star on the way to the manger, one of them said he knew a short cut.
5. Barking dogs do not bite – *while* barking.

112 was für ein ...

TEST YOURSELF : Correct these horrible mistakes

1.	*Was für ein Bier ziehen Sie vor?*	*What* ~~for a~~ beer do you prefer?
2.	*Was für ein Wetter!*	*What* ~~a~~ weather!
3.	*Was für ein Tier ist das?*	*What* ~~an~~ animal is that?
4.	*Für was interessieren Sie sich?*	*What* are you interested *in*?

Joke your way round trouble spots

1. *What a* salesman! He sold the Venus de Milo a spray deodorant.
2. Customer: May I have a pair of alligator shoes?
   Salesman: Certainly. *What* size is your alligator?
3. Tina: I used to be young once.
   Tony: *What a* memory!
4. Anne: I've just come back from the beauty salon.
   Tina: *What a* pity it was closed.
5. A man walked into a police station and said: "I've come about the job that's advertised outside." – "*What* job?" asked the policeman.

113 wenig

TEST YOURSELF : What is it in English?

1. Why are there so *few* women in Parliament?
2. The politician said *little* or nothing.
3. *A few* of the visitors left early.
4. There is *little* hope of finding survivors.

JOKE YOUR WAY round trouble spots

1. Call a meeting at 4.30 on Fridays and you'll get *little* opposition.
2. "Listen boys! When the enemy is only *a few* hundred metres away you may start retreating. Being *a little* lame, I'll leave now."
3. Most of us know how to say nothing – *few* of us know when.
4. A man's credit card was stolen but he decided not to report it because the thief was spending *less* than his wife did.
5. You should be *a little* suspicious of your wife if she asks for her weekly household money in traveller's checks.

114 wenn

TEST YOURSELF : Right or Wrong?

	R	W
1. Don't tell lies ~~if~~ *when* you can use statistics.		✔
2. *If* there's no alternative, there's no problem.	✔	
3. Tact is the art of saying nothing *when* there is nothing to say.	✔	
4. *If* you ~~will~~ look like your passport photo you really need the holiday.		✔
5. I will tell him *when* I ~~will~~ meet him tomorrow.		✔

JOKE YOUR WAY round trouble spots

1. Why does a Lada have heated rear windscreens?
   To keep your hands warm *when* you push it.
2. My wife says she'll leave me *if* I don't throw out my computer. I'll miss her.
3. Education is *when* you read the fine print. Experience is what you get *if* you don't.
4. *If* you want to make a man very angry, tell him you are going to pray for him.

115 werden

TEST YOURSELF : Which word fits best?

1. Wait till the lights *turn* green.
2. The meat *has gone off*. Throw it away.
3. Divorce *is becoming* more and more common.
4. I forgot the keys. I think I'm *growing / getting* old.

JOKE YOUR WAY round trouble spots

1. Doctor, I think I am *going* mad. Every time I ask someone the time I get a different answer.
2. I *get* tired quickly.
3. When I was a boy I was told that anybody could *become* President. I'm beginning to believe it.
4. Is he old? Even his toupee has *turned* grey.

116 wie

TEST YOURSELF : Complete the questions

1. *What* is *Papagei* in English?	It's *parrot.*
2. *How* do you spell *parrot*?	It's spelled with double *r*.
3. *How* is Tom?	He is fine.
4. *What* is your new neighbour *like*?	I hardly know him.

JOKE YOUR WAY round trouble spots

1. It's no fun going to the airline desk to complain about lost luggage only to see the clerk *trying on* my clothes.
2. A true gentleman is someone who knows *how to play* the trumpet but doesn't.
3. "*What's* your new girlfriend *like*?"
4. "Nobody knows *what he looks like*."

117 zuerst

TEST YOURSELF : Put in *at* where necessary

1. He's so shy. *At first* he wouldn't even talk about it.
2. "Do you want a drink?" – "Later, I'll finish my work *first*."

3. Who comes *first*?
4. When did you *first* meet him?
5. I didn't like the job much *at first.*

JOKE YOUR WAY round trouble spots

1. If *at first* you don't succeed, try, try again. Then give up. No use being a damned fool about it.
2. He used to get up out of bed every morning with a headache. And his wife kept telling him, "Honey, it's feet *first*."
3. Bank manager to young house-hunting couple: "*First* you tell me what you can afford."

rororo
© Britta Lembke

Robert Kleinschroth
Anne-Laure Maupai | Dieter Maupai
FRANZÖSISCH
FÜR BÜFFELMUFFEL
rororo